The Waldheim Affair:

DEMOCRACY SUBVERTED

The Waldheim Affair:

DEMOCRACY SUBVERTED

HAROLD H. TITTMANN III

OLIN FREDERICK, INC.
DUNKIRK, NEW YORK

Library of Congress Cataloging-in-Publication Data
Tittmann, Harold
    The Waldheim Affair / by Harold H. Tittmann III

    ISBN: 0-9672357-4-X

To Yveline, Harold, and Oliver

CONTENTS

PREFACE

The campaign to expose Kurt Waldheim as a Nazi war criminal, which came to be known as the "the Waldheim affair," began during his candidacy for the Austrian presidency in 1986. As a lawyer with an interest in World War II history, I routinely followed the developments of the campaign in the newspapers. I had never met Waldheim and knew little about him other than that he had served as Secretary General of the United Nations. But as the Waldheim affair continued to unfold, I began to wonder if an injustice was being done to the man, since it seemed to me unlikely that a young Wehrmacht staff lieutenant with no command authority could have been involved in the serious crimes of which he was accused. I also found it suspicious that, after barring Waldheim from entering the United States for allegedly participating in Nazi persecutions, the U.S. government refused to divulge the evidence on which it had acted. I started to delve into the matter and what I discovered convinced me that it was a story worth telling. I decided to write this book.

Dr. Waldheim had nothing to do with this decision, but he kindly agreed to provide me with much background information and documents. I met him on a number of occasions, the first time in the presidential office in the Hofburg Palace, and later at the offices of the Austrian League for the United Nations which he headed after his retirement. Dr. Waldheim always received me with great courtesy, but I had the impression that, while wishing me luck, he did not believe that my book would ever be published in the United States, partly because of the sensitivity of the subject and partly because I had no credentials as an author.

I owe a debt of gratitude to the numerous persons who helped and encouraged me on my project, above all to John Mapother, a retired CIA veteran who became perhaps the leading expert on the Waldheim affair in the United States. He provided me with countless hours of assistance and support, including a valuable critique of my manuscript.

If this book reads at all well, it is largely due to my friend Larry Gurwin's coaching. Larry, an investigative reporter and author of several books, persuaded me to abandon my lawyer-like style, which I had inevitably acquired during my legal career, in favor of more reader-friendly writing. We spent many hours together going over my drafts, and he provided me with invaluable advice.

Jean Vanwelkenhuyzen and General J. Lawton Collins, who were members of the historians' commission which investigated the allegations against Waldheim, gave generously of their time and provided me with essential background on the workings of that body.

Others whose help and contributions I would like to acknowledge gratefully include: in Austria, Dr. Ralph Scheide, President Waldheim's assistant; Ferdinand Trauttmansdorff of the Austrian Foreign Ministry; and Dr. Hans Koechler of the International Progress Organization; in Washington D.C., Donald Santarelli, Dr. Waldheim's lawyer during the "Watch List" proceedings; Martin Eichtinger, press attaché at the Austrian Embassy; retired ambassador David Popper; David Vladeck, the lawyer who obtained the release of the Justice Department report on Waldheim; Richard Schifter and Mary Mochary, who dealt with the Waldheim affair in the State Department. Judge William P. Clark was the only former senior member of the Reagan administration I could find which was prepared to discuss the Waldheim affair, and he provided me with some useful insights.

And most of all, thanks to Olin Frederick, Inc., which had the courage to publish this book.

INTRODUCTION

By May of 1943, the tide of World War II had turned against the Axis powers. An entire German army had been defeated and captured at Stalingrad after which a steady Russian offensive pushed westward. In the Mediterranean area, Rommel's Afrika Korps had been evicted from North Africa by British and American forces. The Germans and their Italian allies maintained an uneasy control of Yugoslavia and Greece and prepared to defend against a possible Allied landing. At the same time they had to deal with increasingly bold attacks by two rival groups of partisans led by the Communist Tito and the royalist General Mihailovic. A "dirty" war marked by frequent atrocities and reprisals against civilians ensued. In this same month German and Italian troops launched a violent attack on the strongholds of Mihailovic partisans in the rugged mountains of Montenegro. The fighting was fierce and merciless; more than ten thousand partisans were killed, and war crimes no doubt were committed.

During the operation, code-named "Schwartz," the commanding officers convened at the airport of the Montenegrin capital of Podgorica. A military photographer recorded the meeting: the Italian commander, General Escola Roncaglia, is seen conferring with an SS general, Artur Phleps, against a background of dark, mist-shrouded hills. Standing beside them is a young Wehrmacht lieutenant named Kurt Waldheim, the man who served as Secretary-General of the United Nations from 1972 to 1982 and as president of Austria from 1986 to 1992.

While Waldheim was running for the Austrian presidency in 1986, rumors began circulating that he had a hidden Nazi past and had been involved in war crimes, and the Podgorica photograph fell into the hands of the World Jewish Congress (WJC). Determined to prevent the election of a presumed Nazi war criminal, who had allegedly played a role in the Holocaust, the WJC launched a media campaign widely and uncritically reported in *The New York Times* and the press in general. The goal of the WJC was to expose Waldheim's alleged participation in atrocities, including the deportation of Jews from the Balkans. The picture of the tall, dour-looking lieutenant, wearing the classic Wehrmacht uniform including high boots and standing next to an SS general, was widely reproduced in the press. As with Hollywood's black-hatted cowboys, the image was clear: Waldheim was a bad guy. Any doubts in the minds of Americans were dispelled in 1987 when, at the request of the WJC, the U.S. government placed Waldheim, now the elected president of Austria, on a "Watch List" of undesirable aliens barred from entering the United States.

Kurt Waldheim was born in 1918 in Tulln, a pleasant town on the Danube about 35 kilometers northwest of Vienna. His birth coincided with the end of World War I and the break-up of the multinational, multiethnic Austro-Hungarian Empire. The German-speaking part of that empire now became the Republic of Austria, a small, economically feeble nation with less than seven million inhabitants.

Waldheim's father, Walter, was the son of a blacksmith. An ambitious and able man, he became a schoolteacher and after WW I he was appointed superintendent of schools in his district. He and his wife were devout Catholics and supporters of the conservative Christian Social Party which controlled the Austrian government in the 1920s and 30s. When the Nazi movement in Germany planted offshoots in Austria which pushed for a unification of the two countries, the Waldheims openly expressed their disapproval.

No doubt inspired by their father, Kurt and his younger brother and sister, Walther and Gerlinde, were hardworking and successful students. As a teenager, Kurt set his sights on a career in the Austrian foreign service. After finishing high school, he planned to attend the prestigious Consular Academy in Vienna. As a preliminary step towards his goal, in 1936 he volunteered for a year's service in the Austrian army. An enthusiastic horseman, he was assigned to an elite cavalry unit.

Kurt entered the Consular Academy in 1937, a particularly stressful time for his country. Austria was still in the grip of a deep economic depression. Jobs, particularly for the young, were scarce. In Germany, on the other hand, where Hitler was rearming the country, the economy was booming and work plentiful. Since the end of the WW I, a minority of the Austrian population had always been attracted to the idea of unification with Germany. The Austrian Nazi party tried to exploit this tendency for their own ends. After its storm troopers had created civil unrest and murdered the Austrian Premier, the party was declared illegal by the Austrian government and many of its leaders arrested. This, of course, did not please Hitler, who was determined to bring all German-speaking people into the Third Reich. He pressed the Austrian Chancellor, Kurt von Schuschnigg, to accept unification. Schuschnigg tried to gain time by relaxing some of the anti-Nazi measures in Austria, but Hitler was not satisfied. Desperately trying to avoid being taken over by the larger neighbor, Schuschnigg called for a referendum by the Austrian people on the unification issue. The Waldheims participated in the campaign for a vote in favor of an independent Austria. Kurt, while he was passing out leaflets in Vienna, was beaten by a group of young Nazis.

The referendum was to be held March 13, 1938. Since it appeared that a majority of Austrians would vote against unification, Hitler sent in his army on March 12. There was no resistance. Schuschnigg was forced to resign. Kurt remembers watching his mother weep as Schuschnigg, in his farewell radio address, exhorted his listeners to believe in Austria. His Nazi successor, Seyss-Inquart, agreed to the union with Germany, known as the Anschluss. Austria now became "Ostmark," a province of the German Reich.

The Anschluss soon affected the Waldheim family. Kurt's father was arrested on suspicion of anti-Nazi activities, but was released shortly thereafter, as the police were unable to uncover any incriminating evidence. He was, however, dismissed from his post as superintendent of schools and was unable to find new employment in the Nazi-controlled administration. He eventually, through his Catholic Church connections, became involved in training missionaries at a mission near Vienna. After the Anschluss, the Waldheims moved from Tulln to the town of Baden, south of Vienna, where they spent the war years. Although their house was badly damaged in an Allied bombing raid, and both sons were wounded during their military service, the Waldheim family survived the war intact.

In the midst of the political turmoil in 1937 and 1938, Kurt managed to pursue his studies at the Consular Academy, even though his scholarship had been cancelled. The previously relaxed and pleasant Viennese atmosphere at the school gradually changed. As the Nazis assumed control of the administration and student organizations, they made life difficult for Jewish students. Kurt's riding club, along with other Austrian sports organizations, was incorporated in the SA, a Nazi para-military organization.

After the outbreak of World War II, Waldheim was permanently recalled to duty with his cavalry reconnaissance squadron, which had been made part of the German Wehrmacht. His unit participated in the campaign against France, where Waldheim was commissioned as a second lieutenant. Waldheim's unit was transferred to the eastern front in 1941 and participated in the invasion of the Soviet Union. One of the rare cavalry formations of the German army, the unit engaged in the highly dangerous task of flushing out Red Army troops ahead of the infantry. In December 1941 Waldheim was wounded in the leg, and was repatriated to Vienna. After his convalescence, he was declared unfit for further front-line service. Because of his knowledge of Italian, in April 1942 he was

assigned to the German Army command in the Balkans, which needed inter-
preters to coordinate with allied Italian forces. After serving in various Italian
liaison and interpreter positions prior to Italy's surrender, he spent the remaining
war years as a junior staff officer in the German Balkan command. In the course
of extensive home leaves during this period, he managed to complete his studies
and marry his girlfriend, Elizabeth, in 1944.

When the war in Europe ended in May 1945, Waldheim was interned by the
American occupying forces and soon released after his record had been
reviewed. In December 1945, he joined the Austrian Foreign Service and rose
rapidly in its ranks, serving as Austrian ambassador to Canada from 1956 to
1959. In 1968 he was appointed Foreign Minister, which led to his election as
Secretary General of the U.N. in 1971. When he left the U.N. in January 1982,
having been re-elected for a second five-year term in 1977, he had become one
of the most respected and best-known Austrian public figures. Not surprisingly,
the conservative Austrian People's Party chose him as its candidate for the 1986
presidential election.

Though a largely ceremonial position, the Austrian President is the chief of
state, and for the sixty-seven year old Waldheim, this appeared to be a fitting,
pleasant and relatively stress free conclusion to this career. The "happy ending,"
however, was not to be. Because of the war crime accusations and the U.S. government's "Watch List" action, Waldheim's international reputation was severely
damaged, and many of the world's leaders shunned him.

Waldheim consistently denied that he had been involved in any kind of culpable behavior during the war, and the accusations against him hardly sounded
true. They were long on rhetoric and appeared to be based on no meaningful
supporting evidence. Besides, it was unlikely that his alleged participation in war
crimes could have remained undetected for more than forty years when his
background must have been subject to numerous investigations. What is more,
all of the accusations concerned Waldheim's service in the Balkans as a staff
lieutenant with no command authority. It is hard to imagine how he could have
committed the crimes of which he was accused, such as the deportation of Jews,
the murder of British commandos, and massacres of Yugoslav civilians without
such authority.

Yet the U.S. Justice Department, in implementing the "Watch List" decision,
announced to the world that it held irrefutable proof of Waldheim's involvement
in war crimes. The Justice Department refused to divulge the evidence, but who
could doubt the good faith and efficiency of the United States government's

top law enforcement agency? And had not *The New York Times* supported the accusations?

In the United States, Waldheim continues to be regarded as a Nazi war criminal. Is this reputation deserved or was he the victim of a witch hunt?

CHAPTER I

The 1986 Presidential Campaign

As the Austrian presidential election campaign gained momentum in the closing months of 1985, Kurt Waldheim, the candidate of the conservative People's Party, had every reason to be pleased. The polls showed that he had a comfortable lead over his Socialist opponent, Kurt Steyrer, and he could not imagine what could prevent him from becoming Austria's chief of state, the capstone of a distinguished career.

Tall, impressive and always impeccably dressed, Waldheim projected an image of leadership with a dash of urbane charm. Ten years as a top civil servant at the United Nations had taught him how to move with ease in political and diplomatic circles of the highest level. He knew all of the major world leaders. At the same time, he had developed a special rapport with representatives of many of the third-world countries that used the UN as a forum for their views. His experience on the world scene served him well on the campaign trail. Accompanied by Sissy, his attractive wife, Waldheim drew enthusiastic crowds. Austrians were eager to hear and meet their country's most famous international statesman.

The Austrian Socialists, on the other hand, were understandably far from happy with the election prospects. Since the end of World War II, the Austrian presidency had continuously been in the hands of the Socialist Party, the country's largest political group. When Waldheim was selected in 1985 as the candidate of the People's Party, the Socialists realized their tenure was likely to end. Their overall political support was slipping, and Waldheim, Austria's best-known public figure, was a formidable opponent. In 1971, even before his ascension to international prominence, he ran for the presidency on behalf of the People's Party and while he lost, his showing was respectable.

The Socialist leader, Chancellor Fred Sinowatz, believed that Waldheim's campaign could be derailed only by destroying his reputation, proclaimed in the People's Party campaign posters: "Waldheim, an Austrian the world trusts!" Because Waldheim's career in the Austrian Foreign Service and at the United

Nations seemed irreproachable, the best hope for the Socialists lay in uncovering some skeletons from his past, particularly his experiences as a student and soldier during the years Austria was a part of Nazi Germany.[1]

Georg Tidl, an Austrian investigative reporter with close ties to Sinowatz and his chief of staff, Hans Pusch, probed into Waldheim's wartime years and discovered that he had served on the staff of General Alexander Loehr's Army Group E in the Balkans.[2] Army Group E encompassed the German Army units based in Greece and southern Yugoslavia, numbering nearly half a million men. Its headquarters, until the final stages of World War II, was located in the Greek town of Arsakli, outside of Salonika. Loehr, an Austrian and former *Luftwaffe* officer, was executed by the Yugoslavs as a war criminal for his role in the bombing of Belgrade in 1941. Tidl also came across documents indicating that Waldheim may have joined Nazi organizations during his student years.

Whether Tidl was working on his own or under a mandate of the Socialists is unclear, but he evidently kept his Socialists friends informed of his discoveries. A Vienna newspaper, *Plus*, reported that Sinowatz's colleagues, at a party meeting in October 1985, expressed concern over their candidate's diminishing electoral prospects, and Sinowatz told them they should not worry: Waldheim would be "painted brown" by his Nazi past.[3] Sinowatz, not wanting to be viewed as the instigator of the personal attacks on Waldheim, sued the paper for libel. He was unsuccessful, as the newspaper produced a written transcript of Sinowatz's remarks prepared by one of the meeting's participants.

Part of Tidl's file was then leaked to the Viennese weekly magazine, *Profil*, which, at the beginning of 1986, published a story about Waldheim having been on Loehr's staff.[4] The article generated little interest in Austria. After all, why was Waldheim's service as a lieutenant on the staff of Army Group E of any particular significance?

The trial balloon had not produced the desired effect. Consequently, Socialist leaders decided that stronger measures were necessary to damage Waldheim's reputation, but they realized they had to be careful. Engaging in personal attacks might work to the Socialists' disadvantage. It would be better if the assault on Waldheim appeared to come from another source, preferably from abroad. This was risky. Austrian voters would react badly should the hidden hand of the Socialists be exposed, especially if the interference were to be orchestrated from abroad. Obviously the choice of an appropriate ally was crucial. The most likely candidates were the major international Jewish organizations, since these groups had an understandable motivation to expose a Nazi war criminal. The Socialists chose the New York-based World Jewish Congress (WJC).[5]

The WJC was not the largest Jewish group, but it derived its considerable influence from the key role its prestigious founder, Nahum Goldmann, had played in the creation of the State of Israel. The WJC's mission was to protect Jewish interests in general, and it had representatives throughout the world. Its influence grew after Edgar Bronfman Sr., head of the Seagram liquor conglomerate, became president in 1981. One of the world's richest men, Bronfman had extensive contacts with U.S. and Israeli political and media circles and was militantly involved in Jewish causes, such as the emigration of Soviet Jewry. The Socialists presumed that Bronfman would favor the exposure of the Nazi and war-criminal past of as prominent a figure as Waldheim. In addition, the parents of the WJC director general, Israel Singer, had suffered under the Nazis following the annexation of Austria; Singer would probably support an attack on Waldheim. The Austrian Socialists seemed to have made the right choice as the WJC not only proved to be interested in going after Waldheim, but also did so with extraordinary zeal, leading to unexpected consequences for the Socialists.

The conduit for the Socialists to the WJC was Leon Zelman, a well-known Jewish personality in Vienna and a friend of Israel Singer. The Socialists asked him to approach the WJC. In late January 1986, Zelman met Singer at a WJC meeting in Tel Aviv and told him that Waldheim may have had a Nazi past. With scarcely a moment of hesitation, Singer sent his general counsel, Eli Rosenbaum, to Vienna to look into the allegations against Waldheim.[6]

For Rosenbaum, an energetic young attorney, the assignment was particularly appropriate. Following his graduation from Harvard Law School in 1980, he had spent three years on the staff of the Justice Department's Office of Special Investigations whose mission was to seek out and deport Nazi war criminals residing in the United States. "Nazi hunting" became his primary goal in life, to which he applied himself with a passion marked by a tendency to jump to unsupported conclusions.

After joining the WJC as general counsel, Rosenbaum found himself back in the Nazi-hunting business although the Waldheim affair would prove to be far more complicated than those he had dealt with at OSI. The new assignment required knowledge of German military procedures and the capacity to analyze German Army documents. Despite his lack of experience in these areas, Rosenbaum became the chief executor of the WJC campaign against Waldheim.[7]

In his 1993 book, *Betrayal*, Rosenbaum described his Vienna mission in melodramatic and sometimes unintentionally comical terms.[8] Upon arrival, Rosenbaum was put in touch with a mysterious individual possessing an "interesting" file on Waldheim's early years. This man agreed to talk only if his identity were kept secret. Rosenbaum and Schuller (the informant's pseudonym) arranged a discreet meeting at dusk in a deserted Viennese park. Schuller carried a rolled newspaper under his arm to identify himself. The pair proceeded to a nearby vacant office, where Schuller, between numerous gulps of vodka, revealed to an enthralled Rosenbaum documents which showed that Waldheim may have been a member of several Nazi organizations when he was a student in Vienna before the war. The documents also indicated that in 1943 and 1944 Waldheim had served on the staff of General Loehr's Army Group E in the Balkans. The key item Schuller produced was a 1943 photo purporting to show Waldheim at a meeting of German and Italian officers at the Podgorica airfield in Montenegro. It proved, Schuller asserted, that Waldheim had lied about his service in the Balkans. He had claimed in various publications that, after recovering from his Russian-front wound in 1942, he had returned to duty only in 1944 when the war was nearly over. Schuller asked Rosenbaum to take the photo to the United States to have it authenticated. Rosenbaum hesitated. He was afraid that he might be thrown in jail if the Austrian police searched him on his departure from Vienna airport and found the compromising photo. Rosenbaum decided to take the risk. He cleared the airport checkpoint without incident, but claimed that the experience left him drained.

Schuller's identity has generated much speculation in Austria. According to Rosenbaum, Schuller had close links to the Austrian Socialist Party and admitted that, for political reasons, he had collected a considerable amount of information about Waldheim's early years.[9] Rumors circulated in Vienna that Schuller was an independent researcher who thought he could sell his story to the beleaguered Socialists for a hefty price. The Socialists, unwilling or unable to pay, might then have steered him to the deeper pockets of the WJC and its wealthy president.

Rosenbaum was pressed by Austrian reporters to reveal his source but steadfastly refused to do so. To this day, Schuller's identity has remained a secret.

Armed with the information Schuller had given him and the precious Podgorica photo, Rosenbaum returned to WJC headquarters in New York and proposed to his superiors an investigation into Waldheim's student and wartime years. Rosenbaum later explained in his book that the photo had provided him with a clue as to why Waldheim had covered up his Balkan service: one of the German officers at the meeting, Artur Phleps, was "a full-fledged SS-*Gruppenfuehrer*," commander of the Prinz Eugen SS division which allegedly committed atrocities against Yugoslav civilians. For Rosenbaum, mere proximity to Phleps implied guilt, regardless of Waldheim's role at the meeting.[10]

The photo became a key element in the WJC campaign against Waldheim.

The image of the tall, young German officer provided a convenient prop for those editorial writers and cartoonists who would depict him as a Nazi war criminal. He was even linked to the SS on the basis of his cavalry boots, even though such boots were a standard feature of a Wehrmacht officer's uniform.[11] To Waldheim, the exploitation of this photo would come to symbolize the dishonest tactics of his enemies.

Within a few hours, Singer and Bronfman had authorized Rosenbaum to proceed with the investigation of Waldheim.[12] In less than a month, the WJC generated a front-page story in America's most prestigious newspaper, *The New York Times*, which insinuated that Waldheim had been involved in war crimes and was a former Nazi. From then on, the WJC's pursuit of Waldheim received extensive coverage in the media. The Austrian presidential elections, an event normally attracting little interest outside of Austria, suddenly gained international attention. The U.S. press, sensing that a major Nazi war criminal story was unfolding, gave the elections full coverage, accompanied by editorials and op-ed pieces that were uniformly anti-Waldheim.

How had the WJC managed to engineer such a public relations coup? Its principals knew that to launch an effective attack on Waldheim press involvement was essential, and that if *The New York Times* could be persuaded to carry the story, worldwide coverage would almost certainly follow. The WJC happened to have close contacts with the *Times*. After seeing the Schuller materials, the editors assigned the story to their Rome-based reporter, John Tagliabue. At WJC insistence, the *Times* agreed not to reveal Schuller's identity. Rosenbaum, evidently viewing Austria as a country addicted to political assassinations, surmised in his book that Schuller may have placed his life in Rosenbaum's hands through his disclosures and that the responsibility of hiding Schuller's identity weighed heavily on him.[13]

Rosenbaum flew back to Vienna at the end of February. There he he met with the *Times* reporter and Schuller, who had in the meantime dug up some additional information on Waldheim's activities in the Balkans. Closeted in Schuller's house, the three men examined Schuller's file and agreed on a game plan. Tagliabue would request an interview with Waldheim who would assume that the *Times* wanted the story on the Austrian presidential elections. The interview, however, would focus entirely on Waldheim's war years. The three men expected that Waldheim, unaware that Tagliabue had been given access to information about those years, could be trapped into giving demonstrably untrue answers. Tagliabue planned to confront Waldheim with the Podgorica photo which an ex-CIA document expert had authenticated for the WJC. Rosenbaum, convinced that Waldheim would try to cover up his Balkan service, expected him to fall into the trap by dismissing it as a fake.[14]

Upon his return to Italy, Tagliabue contacted Waldheim, who readily agreed to grant him an interview on March 3. On that day, the Austrian weekly *Profil* published an article about Waldheim's alleged Nazi affiliations during his student days as well as certain details of his Balkan service. The Nazi affiliation accusation stemmed from the discovery, probably by Tidl, of Waldheim's military service record (*Wehrstammkarte*) in the Austrian military archives. On this document, under the heading "organization memberships," appeared the notations "SA. N.S.D.S.B.," referring to the SA (*Sturmabteilung*, a Nazi paramilitary organization) and to the Nazi Student Union. This was the Nazi "past" into which Sinowatz had proposed to dip Waldheim.

With Waldheim's approval, Hubertus Czernin, a reporter for *Profil*, and Ferdinand Trauttmansdorff, an Austrian diplomat detached to work on Waldheim's campaign staff, inspected Waldheim's file in the Austrian archives. Trauttmansdorff was at first shocked by the references to the Nazi organizations, and considered abandoning the Waldheim team for fear of negative effects on his future diplomatic career. Waldheim insisted he had not voluntarily joined either organization. Reassured, Trauttmansdorff decided to stay on.[15]

The Waldheim personnel files also contained a document that specifically testified to Waldheim's anti-Nazi views: A 1940 communication from the Nazi Provincial (*Gau*) office responsible for Waldheim's hometown to the Justice Ministry. The Ministry had inquired about any objections to Waldheim's possible appointment to the judicial service. The *Gau* office replied that the Waldheim family, including Kurt, was regarded as hostile to the Nazi movement but that due to Kurt's good record as a soldier, the *Gau* authorities would not object to a judicial service appointment.[16]

In his interview with Tagliabue, Waldheim denied having knowingly joined Nazi organizations but readily admitted serving in the German Army in the Balkans. When Tagliabue confronted him with the Podgorica photo, he acknowledged that it was genuine and that he appeared in it. He explained he had attended the meeting as an interpreter because Italian officers participated.

Rosenbaum was obviously disappointed. "The reaction was not quite what we had expected," he wrote in his book.[17] While Waldheim may have been surprised that Tagliabue wanted primarily to discuss events that had occurred nearly fifty years before, he showed no reluctance in answering the reporter's questions.

Tagliabue's article, headlined "Files Show Kurt Waldheim Served Under War

Criminal," appeared on the front page of *The New York Times* on March 4, 1986, accompanied by a large reproduction of the Podgorica photo. The text, however, did not point out that the war criminal in question, General Loehr, was convicted primarily in connection with the bombing of Belgrade in 1941. The article noted Waldheim's presence at the Podgorica meeting with General Phleps, whose division, claimed the article rightly, "was guilty of some of the most brutal crimes against civilians."

Tagliabue wrote that the "potentially most embarrassing disclosures concern Mr. Waldheim's presence in Salonika in the spring of 1943" when the Jews of Salonika were deported to German concentration camps. Waldheim denied having anything to do with the deportations. The leading expert on the deportation of Greek Jews, Professor of History Hagen Fleischer of the University of Crete, supported him in this. Fleischer told Reuters he knew the names of all those involved in rounding up Jews in Salonika, and Waldheim was not among them. Waldheim, Fleischer said, "had nothing to do with Greek Jewry."[18] Nevertheless, Tagliabue's article led to accusations that Waldheim had participated in the Holocaust.

Tagliabue also claimed that Waldheim had not been forthcoming about his past because he had not referred to his service in the Balkans in his recent book, *In the Eye of the Storm*, or in a 1980 letter to Congressman Solarz. Tagliabue did not mention that the German version of the book had referred to such service,[19] even though Rosenbaum and Schuller were aware of this fact[20] and normally would have raised it during the reporter's briefing. Tagliabue may not have been particularly impressed by Schuller's and Rosenbaum's war-crime allegations. He surmised in his article that the "cover up" could ultimately turn out to be the most serious accusation against Waldheim. It was, in any event, a convenient fallback position. When reporters pressed Rosenbaum in the early stages of the campaign against Waldheim, his standard retort was that he was not now accusing Waldheim of being a war criminal but rather of lying about his past by claiming that his military service had ended in 1942 following his injury on the Eastern front.[21]

The Tagliabue article was the opening salvo in the WJC campaign—a campaign which was directed, seemingly at upsetting Waldheim's bid for the Austrian Presidency. The WJC, however, publicly denied trying to influence the Austrian voters. On March 5, 1986 Singer told *The New York Times* that the disclosures were not timed to coincide with the election campaign. "There has been a rumor mill on Waldheim for years, and we just got around to sending our legal counsel to Austria to take a look around. It had nothing to do with the Austrian elections," Singer asserted.[22]

In the following days, the WJC attacked Waldheim in a series of news releases reiterating the allegations published in the Tagliabue article. The WJC focused on his receipt of a Croatian decoration known as the King Zvonimir Medal, ostensibly granted for bravery under enemy fire. For the WJC, this decoration demonstrated the importance of Waldheim's role in the Balkan conflict and belied his claim that he had been declared unfit for combat duty. In one of its releases, the WJC announced that its president Edgar Bronfman, had called on Jewish communities in seventy countries to assist in investigating Waldheim.[23]

The WJC soon realized that its efforts had failed to hurt Waldheim's electoral chances. On the contrary, a poll taken during the week following the Tagliabue article showed that Waldheim's lead had widened, and he seemed to be benefiting from a wave of sympathy among Austrians as a result of the WJC attacks.[24] An Austrian reporter had reviewed the records of Loehr's army group at the German military archives in Freiburg and had found nothing incriminating. He noted that Waldheim had served as an adjutant in the military intelligence branch of the army group headquarters.[25] The Austrian voters evidently did not consider Waldheim's Balkan service as proof of any wrongdoing on his part.

Israel Singer had reached much the same conclusion. Recognizing that the WJC campaign against Waldheim needed to produce evidence of Waldheim's personal involvement in war crimes, Singer instructed Rosenbaum to search German army records at the National Archives in Washington and authorized him to obtain the assistance of military historians for that purpose. Rosenbaum hired Robert Herzstein, a professor of history at the University of South Carolina who had written several books about Nazi Germany.[26]

Herzstein spent a week at the National Archives and found a number of German Army documents relating to Waldheim. In addition, he came across a U.S. Army report indicating that Waldheim, at the request of the Yugoslav government, had been listed in 1948 as a suspected war criminal by the UN War Crimes Commission.[27]

All of a sudden, the WJC attacks on Waldheim, which had been long on invective but short on proof, seemed spectacularly vindicated. Rosenbaum obtained Singer's approval to issue an immediate press release on the UNWCC story despite the lack of any information concerning the background for the war crimes listing or of an answer to the obvious question of why the Yugoslavs had failed to pursue their case. Waldheim immediately denied any knowledge of the

UNWCC listing, and the Yugoslav authorities, obviously embarrassed, refused to comment. The story was not the bombshell the WJC had expected.

On March 25, the WJC held a press conference at its New York offices to make public the results of Herzstein's research. Herzstein, who had completed his mission for the WJC and was about to return to his teaching duties, personally reported on his findings at the national Archives. He declared that the German Army records showed that Waldheim had served as an intelligence officer on Loehr's staff and that he and another lieutenant were responsible for preparing the morning and evening reports on the military situation—reports based on a variety of sources including prisoner interrogations. Herzstein had found a reference to British prisoners of war in one of Waldheim's reports. This reference would later lead to additional charges. Next, he noted that Waldheim had been involved—it was not clear in what capacity—in the so-called Kozara campaign against Yugoslav partisans for which he had been awarded the King Zvonimir Medal. Herzstein claimed that in this campaign the Germans and their Croatian allies had massacred their opponents. Finally, he described Operation Schwartz, the subject of the Podgorica meeting Waldheim attended, as a particularly brutal operation against partisans by the Prinz Eugen SS Division. Even though Herzstein had found no evidence linking Waldheim personally to criminal acts, Rosenbaum declared to the assembled reporters:

> In my experience as a federal prosecutor, rarely did I see documents of such devastating impact as those that we are making available today. I cannot imagine that there is a single prosecutor in the world who would reach any conclusion other than that this documentary evidence is of a character and weight that, at a minimum, compels the initiation of a major criminal investigation... We call on the government of Austria, in particular, to launch such an investigation with all deliberate speed.[28]

Rosenbaum did not explain what he had in mind as the "maximum" that the documentation might compel. Some reporters were skeptical. They asked Rosenbaum whether the WJC was accusing Waldheim of being a war criminal directly involved in atrocities. Rosenbaum admitted that the WJC was not prepared to make such an assertion. *The New York Post*, however, had no qualms. Its story on Herzstein's press conference was headlined, "Papers Show Waldheim Was SS Butcher."

At the close of the press conference, Singer, describing Waldheim as a liar and a Nazi, once again denied that the WJC was trying to force the withdrawal of Waldheim's candidacy, but, as Rosenbaum admitted, no one was deceived.[29] Any pretense of non-interference had in fact disappeared when Singer, in an interview published in *Profil* on March 24, 1986, threatened Austria and the Austrian people with dire consequences if Waldheim were elected president. Singer asserted that Waldheim's first year in office would be no honeymoon, and that the accusations against him would haunt and follow not only the president, but every Austrian. He predicted that the country's tourist industry and foreign trade would suffer. Waldheim supporters and the Austrian press took full advantage of Singer's remarks to denounce the WJC interference in Austrian domestic politics. The People's Party campaign posters proclaimed, "We Austrians will elect whom we want!"

Next, the WJC requested the incumbent Austrian president, Rudolf Kirchschlaeger, to review the nearly 500 National Archives documents it had uncovered and inform the Austrian people of their content. Kirchschlaeger, a lawyer by background, agreed to do so.[30] His review would also include the UNWCC file, which had in the meantime been released to the Austrian government. He reported the results of his review in a television broadcast on April 22, declaring that if he were in the position of prosecutor, he would not dare bring charges against Waldheim on the basis of the UNWCC file, because the allegations of the only cited witness were not credible. As for the WJC documents, he found none linking Waldheim to any criminal act, although he opined that Waldheim must have been aware of reprisal actions. He appealed for calm on both sides of the Atlantic and said that he was pleased that the pace of the WJC attacks on Waldheim appeared to have subsided.

The lull in the storm was only temporary. The WJC was not about to call off its campaign, supported as it was by the American media and politicians such as Senator Daniel Patrick Moynihan of New York. Indeed, Moynihan declared, Waldheim was a liar and was not "welcome in the United States, as president of Austria or as anything."[31] Editorialists and op-ed writers called on Waldheim to drop out of the presidential race, urging Austrians, in any event, not to vote for him.[32]

During the following weeks, Rosenbaum himself conducted additional searches at the National Archives but failed to produce a "smoking gun." The chronology of Waldheim's Balkan service, which gradually became established through WJC efforts, Austrian researchers, and Waldheim himself, showed that he had served in a number of different places including Tirana, Athens, and Bosnia, in addition to his primary assignment as an intelligence officer at

Loehr's headquarters at Arsakli, Greece. Clearly Waldheim was not in the Salonika area when the mass deportation of Jews took place in the spring of 1943,[33] and the WJC stopped trying to connect him to that event. The Balkan campaign, largely a struggle between Germans and Greek and Yugoslav partisans, was a "dirty" war, and there was no doubt that war crimes had been committed. Although the WJC attempted to link Waldheim personally to such crimes, the effort faced a major obstacle: as a junior staff officer, Waldheim had no command authority.[34] Nevertheless, the WJC needed to maintain a continuous flow of accusations to keep its campaign alive, at least in the United States, as it was collapsing in Austria.

To the chagrin of the WJC, the Austrian press defended Waldheim and denounced WJC "excesses." Polls showed that the Austrian voters were still not buying the WJC accusations. The Socialists distanced themselves from the war-crime charges, concentrating instead on issues of Waldheim's credibility. Even worse, Simon Wiesenthal, the well-known Nazi hunter, refused to rally around the WJC flag and spoke in support of Waldheim. Expressing skepticism about the UN war-crimes file, Wiesenthal deplored the WJC campaign, which he forecast would foment anti-Semitism in Austria. He declared it unjust to accuse a man publicly of being a war criminal without proof.[35]

Wiesenthal was not the only Jewish personality in Austria concerned by the prospect of a rise in anti-Semitism. The Israeli ambassador in Vienna, Michael Elizur, sent a cable to his foreign ministry recommending that Prime Minister Shimon Peres should talk to his friend Bronfman about the "great and unnecessary damage" to Jewish interests in Austria caused by the WJC campaign.[36] Elizur's request was rejected, but it was highly unlikely that anyone could have persuaded Bronfman to stop. The president of Vienna's Jewish community told Singer that this intemperate attack on Waldheim was making life difficult for Austrian Jews. Singer reportedly asked how many Jews lived in Austria, and when told that there were only 6,000, said, "Well, let them emigrate."[37]

The specter of a rise in anti-Semitism during the presidential campaign was a particularly unfortunate consequence of the WJC attacks on Waldheim. These attacks caused anxiety among the survivors of Austria's formerly large and thriving Jewish community, as irresponsible elements among the Austrian press blamed "Jews" for Waldheim's problems.[38] For its part, the WJC considered any criticism of its actions equivalent to attacking Jews in general. Thus when Waldheim declared that the WJC was running a smear campaign against him, the WJC accused him of anti-Semitism.[39] Waldheim never indulged in any racist rhetoric. Subsequently, a prominent English Jew and Austrian émigré, Lord Weidenfeld, testified that Waldheim was not anti-Semitic.[40]

Constrained by the rigors and the protocol of the election campaign, Waldheim defended himself against the WJC accusations as best he could. He expressed regret that he had not been more explicit in his books with respect to his Balkan service, a service he then tried to clarify.[41] In doing so, he gave the wrong dates for some of his assignments. These lapses he later attributed to his inability to remember all the details of events that had occurred more than forty years before. His critics, however, accused him of pursuing a cover-up.

From the beginning, Waldheim repeatedly denied that he had been involved in war crimes. In the United States, Waldheim's denials were met with a standard rejoinder: because Waldheim had not discussed his Balkan service in his writings, he must have been hiding his guilt. Obviously, Waldheim could not prove specifically that he was *not* hiding something. And so, ironically, this absence of evidence permitted the WJC and the U.S. media to portray Waldheim as a villain.

Most Austrians, however, believed that the only fair approach was to consider Waldheim innocent until proven guilty. German Chancellor Helmut Kohl shared this view and described Waldheim's enemies as "arrogant," but he was virtually the only public figure outside of Austria who expressed support. Israeli Foreign Minister Yitzhak Shamir declared that Waldheim's election would be a "political, diplomatic, and human" tragedy.[42]

In the May election Waldheim obtained the largest number of votes, but an environmental candidate picked up a few percentage points, and with 49.6 percent of the vote Waldheim just missed a clear majority. A runoff election was scheduled for June 8th.

In the month that followed, the campaign against Waldheim continued unabated. The highlight was the press conference the WJC held on May 14. Its purpose was to disclose an intelligence report prepared by Waldheim on October 12, 1944. According to the WJC, this report implicated him in massacres of civilians in the Stip-Kocane sector of Macedonia. Waldheim had noted in the report that partisan forces were approaching that area. Two days later, German troops of the Twenty-Second Infantry Division burned down several neighboring villages, killing a number of civilians. After the war, the Yugoslavs executed the German captain in charge of the troops as the war criminal responsible for having ordered the reprisals.

Rosenbaum announced to the reporters that "at a minimum" Waldheim had recklessly endangered human life by reporting information he knew would result in atrocities. Rosenbaum again did not explain what the "maximum" might have been, and he failed to point out that Waldheim's report was based on information submitted by the unit in the field that committed the massacre. Waldheim was not the source. WJC officials, stating that the documents would be helpful in bringing Waldheim to trial, again called on the governments of Austria, Yugoslavia, and Greece to initiate criminal investigations against Waldheim.[43]

The WJC passed the Stip-Kocane documents to Israeli Minister of Justice Yitshak Moda'i, who became an eager, and imprudent, participant in the campaign against Waldheim. Interviewed by the BBC on May 23, Moda'i asserted that Israel had enough evidence to put Waldheim on trial as an accessory to Nazi war crimes. This evidence, Moda'i said, consisted of "proof" that Waldheim passed on information that led to "liquidation actions," hinting that witnesses might be produced to prove Waldheim's personal involvement in war crimes.[44]

According to an Israel Radio report, a committee in the Israeli Justice Department had also concluded that Waldheim committed crimes against Jews in World War II.[45] Waldheim supporters promptly accused the Israeli government of launching a witch hunt, but Moda'i was undeterred. Although he admitted on June 4 in an interview on Israel Radio that the government had been unable to turn up any firm evidence of Waldheim's personal involvement in war crimes,[46] he declared at a press conference in New York on June 6 that an elderly Greek Jew, Moshe Mayuni, now living in Israel, had described to Israeli investigators how he had watched helplessly as Waldheim beat his brother to death in Toanina after stealing gold from him.[47] That sensational accusation soon faded away when proof surfaced that Waldheim had been on sick leave in Vienna on the date of the alleged murder, and nothing further was heard from Mr. Mayuni. Rosenbaum, having experienced the unreliability of Holocaust-survivor testimony during his years at OSI, persuaded his bosses at WJC to maintain a prudent silence on the matter.[48]

On June 8, Waldheim was elected by 53.9 percent of the votes, a better result than the polls had predicted. Political commentators from both parties agreed that the accusations of the WJC had helped Waldheim's campaign. The strategy of the Austrian Socialists to prevent Waldheim's election, with the help of the WJC, had indeed backfired.

The Israeli reaction to Waldheim's victory was predictably negative, and at times even hysterical. President Chaim Herzog omitted sending the customary congratulatory telegram,[49] and the government recalled the Israeli ambassador to Austria, Michael Elizur, indicating that Israel would not have an ambassador in Vienna as long as Waldheim remained president.[50] Holocaust survivors demonstrated in front of the Austrian embassy in Tel Aviv, and Rabbi Meir Kahane ripped an Austrian flag to shreds in the Israeli Parliament, referring to Waldheim as a "Nazi pig." An Israeli government official described Waldheim's election as "a nightmare for every Jew."[51] Moda'i declared to the Parliament that if Waldheim were in Israel, a police investigation would be opened against him as a war-crimes suspect.[52]

In the United States, President Reagan congratulated Waldheim on his victory, but more than one hundred members of Congress requested him not to send an official representative to Waldheim's inauguration.[53] The U.S. ambassador in Vienna, Ronald Lauder, a prominent New York Jew and supporter of the WJC, did not attend the inauguration.[54] The Austrian government greatly resented the snub. U.S. Jewish organizations expressed dismay at Waldheim's election, and newspapers were full of critical commentaries. In *The New York Times*, Anthony Lewis urged private individuals to express their moral revulsion at the choice of the Austrian electorate,[55] while Edgar Bronfman Sr. equated that choice to "an amnesty for the Holocaust."[56]

The WJC did not end its attacks on Waldheim with his election. The organization was determined to make life as difficult as possible for the newly-elected Austrian president and hoped to involve the U.S. government in this effort. In March 1986, Rosenbaum, on behalf of the WJC, had requested Attorney General Edwin Meese to place Waldheim "as soon as possible" on the Watch List of aliens barred from entering the United States because of his participation in Nazi persecutions.[57] Meese asked the Office of Special Investigations, the agency responsible for such matters in the Justice Department, to examine the case. Reports soon appeared in the press that OSI had recommended placing Waldheim on the Watch List, but that the attorney general would not make a decision until after the Austrian elections.[58] Thus the Watch List action, equivalent to a finding of guilt by the U.S. government, hung like a sword of Damocles over Waldheim as he began his term as president. Although the WJC continued its media attacks on Waldheim, the focus shifted to the Justice Department and specifically OSI, which became a key player in the Waldheim affair.

CHAPTER II

The Office of Special Investigations

In the early 1970s, Elisabeth Holtzman, an energetic congresswoman representing a heavily Jewish district in Brooklyn, N.Y., began looking into allegations appearing in the press that the United States was harboring thousands of Nazi war criminals who had managed to enter the country after World War II. Her attention focused on the Immigration and Naturalization Service of the Department of Justice. In cooperation with the State Department, INS monitored the admission of aliens into the United States and their eligibility for U.S. citizenship.[1] The legislative mandate of the INS was the Immigration and Nationality Act. This act listed numerous categories of unwanted foreigners, among them: drug addicts, alcoholics, prostitutes, polygamists, persons coming to the United States to engage in any immoral sexual act, and persons involved in Nazi-related persecutions.[2] The last category came about as a result of a 1978 amendment named after the congresswoman.

More specifically, the INS maintained a Watch List of aliens deemed excludable under the Act. It was also responsible for the denaturalization and deportation of persons who illegally obtained their citizenship by concealing their Nazi past on their visa applications.

Holtzman did not like what she saw at INS. She was convinced that not enough was being done to locate and expel Nazi war criminals. In 1977, at her instigation, INS set up a Special Litigation Unit specifically devoted to this purpose, but in Holtzman's view, the results did not improve sufficiently. In 1978, she became head of the House Immigration Subcommittee. From this position, she used her influence to press President Carter's attorney general, Griffin Bell, to remove Nazi-hunting from the jurisdiction of INS and assign it to an organization within the Justice Department itself. In March 1979, Bell agreed to set up a new unit within the Justice Department's Criminal Division with the impressive-sounding name of Office of Special Investigations. The OSI would report to a deputy assistant attorney general.[3]

OSI began operating in the summer of 1979 in a K Street office building in downtown Washington. Initially, it had a budget of 2.3 million dollars and a staff which grew to fifty people including twenty lawyers, seven historians, and four investigators.[4] During its formative years, OSI was run by Allan A. Ryan Jr., a young Justice Department attorney who would play a role in the Waldheim affair.

OSI's sponsors hoped that at long last the hunt for hidden Nazis would move into high gear, but the OSI mission was hampered from the beginning by a number of constraints. Although part of the Criminal Division, OSI could not prosecute Nazi war criminals. The fact remained that their crimes had not been committed on U.S. soil. OSI had to rely instead on the administrative and civil procedures of denaturalization and deportation in the hope that other countries would mete out appropriate punishment. For the dedicated young lawyers such as Eli Rosenbaum, who had joined the staff of OSI with a burning desire to bring perpetrators of World War II atrocities to justice, this limitation was frustrating.

The second and far more serious problem OSI faced was the possibility that the thousands of Nazi criminals presumed to be living in the United States did not exist in those numbers or, to the extent they did exist, did not commit misdeeds of sufficient importance to merit prosecution. In any event, nearly forty years after the end of the war, potential OSI targets were inevitably growing older and fewer.

As it turned out, the majority of INS and OSI cases involved low-level guards, primarily Poles, Ukrainians, and Balts, who had been drafted into German service following the 1941 invasion of the Soviet Union.[5] Often OSI was unable to show that the individuals personally committed any crimes, but their failure to disclose their service as camp guards on their immigration applications was sufficient to strip them of their U.S. citizenship. They could then be deported under the Holtzman Amendment.[6] This vaguely worded law provided for the deportation or exclusion from the United States of anyone who, on behalf of Nazi Germany, "ordered, incited, assisted, or otherwise participated in the persecution of any person because of race, religion, national origin, or political opinion." One OSI function was to identify nonresident aliens falling within the provisions of the Holtzman Amendment and have them placed on the INS Watch List.

Despite the support OSI enjoyed in Congress and in the Jewish community, it was under pressure from the beginning of its existence, to justify its substantial budget and fend off critics who questioned the value of spending money to pursue elderly ex-concentration camp guards. OSI had to produce results for its sponsors who had great expectations. Successful prosecutions were therefore essential, particularly in those rare cases involving suspects of greater rank or villainy, and thus of greater public interest. Three examples illustrate how OSI pursued this goal prior to taking on the Waldheim case.

1. The Walus case[7]

The INS initiated proceedings against Frank Walus in 1977, which OSI assumed responsibility for in 1979. Walus was a Pole who immigrated to the United States in 1959, settled in Chicago, and became a U.S. citizen in 1970. In 1974, Simon Wiesenthal tipped off the Justice Department that Walus had turned in several Jews to the Gestapo in Poland during the war. The INS launched an investigation and asked the Israeli police to find possible witnesses. Through ads placed in newspapers in Israel, the police came up with a number of Holocaust survivors who were prepared to testify that Walus had indeed been in Poland during the war, and, as a member of the Gestapo and SS, had brutalized and murdered Jews. Denaturalization proceedings were brought against Walus in the Federal District Court in Chicago amid sensational coverage in the press and television. Israeli judicial authorities fanned the flames with leaks to a Chicago newspaper which quoted them as claiming that the case against Walus was "airtight." Allan Ryan later admitted, however, that the case should never have been brought.

The government relied on testimony regarding events that took place thirty-five years earlier by witnesses recruited through newspaper ads in Israel, a procedure that obviously risked producing people willing to testify at a Nazi war-crime trial for motives not necessarily related to the discovery of the truth. The witnesses identified Walus as a man who, while wearing SS and Gestapo uniforms, had committed numerous atrocities against Jews including the shootings of a woman and her two daughters, a group of children, and even a hunchback.

At the time of the alleged crimes, though, Walus had been a frail seventeen-year-old-boy, slightly over five feet tall, hardly the stuff for the SS and Gestapo. Moreover, although the judge did not allow Walus's lawyer to discredit it, the testimony of the witnesses had disturbing discrepancies, particularly in descriptions of Walus. More importantly, Walus was able to prove through documents and witnesses that he had spent the war years as a forced farm laborer in Bavaria. Nevertheless, the judge ruled that Walus was a Nazi war criminal and stripped him of his citizenship. Walus's lawyer, however, found additional evidence corroborating Walus's presence in Bavaria, and he appealed.

By this time, OSI had been formed and had become responsible for the Walus case, but this development did not affect the prosecutors' determination to expel Walus from the United States. Although the fact that they were pursuing the wrong man was growing more evident, they vigorously contested the appeal. In a decision dated February 13, 1980, the Court of Appeals ordered a new trial, stating that the evidence would almost certainly compel a different result. At that point, the OSI should have known that the game was up, but for nine additional months, while OSI "reexamined" the evidence, Walus had to endure the menace of a new trial and possibility of eventual deportation. Even worse, he had to live with the stigma of being a proven Nazi war criminal of the worst kind.

On November 26, 1980, Allan Ryan finally announced that the government was dropping its case against Walus. He did not admit that a mistake had been made or that Walus was innocent. Instead, he cited the requirement that the government's evidence be sufficiently clear and convincing to revoke a person's citizenship. He concluded, "In this case, the evidence plainly falls short of that standard." The implication of possible guilt angered Walus. He was never able to shake off the Nazi stigma. The OSI decision also upset Lieutenant Colonel Menachem Russek of the Israeli national police who had produced the Israeli witnesses. Russek sent a letter of protest to Allan Ryan, complaining that the decision to drop the case against Walus was an affront to the witnesses.[8]

OSI was not responsible for the decision to prosecute ("persecute" may be a more accurate term) Frank Walus, although it needlessly prolonged his ordeal. It also certainly did not merit the praise of the judge who, in dismissing the case, referred to "a worthy and courageous government and its servants who are able and willing to investigate evidence favorable to an accused." In truth, a decision by the Court of Appeals was needed to achieve this result.

Ryan claimed in his 1984 book, *Quiet Neighbors*, that the Walus case had taught OSI a number of lessons, including the need to adopt more stringent procedures for locating witnesses and to beware of cases where no documents could back up the charges. He asserted, "When the U.S. government charges a person with having been a Nazi war criminal, it had better be right, because if it is wrong, the consequences are disastrous." According to Ryan, the most important lesson to be learned from the Walus case was that "an office like OSI was needed not only to prosecute the guilty but to protect the innocent."[9] If in fact OSI ever learned these lessons, its prosecution of a retired autoworker from Cleveland accused of being "Ivan the Terrible" would show that they were quickly forgotten.

2. The Demjanjuk case[10]

John Demjanjuk was born in the Ukraine in 1920. He was serving in the Soviet Army at the time of the German invasion. The Germans captured him in 1942 and toward the end of the war he was recruited to serve in the Vlasov Army, made up of Soviet prisoners of war who were prepared to fight alongside the German Army on the Russian front. In 1952, he immigrated to the United States as a displaced person, settled down with his family in a suburb of Cleveland, Ohio, and became an American citizen.

In 1976, a Ukrainian newspaper in New York with close links to the Soviets published a list of alleged war criminals living in the United States. The roster included Demjanjuk, as well as a Feodor Fedorenko, who had allegedly served as a guard at the Treblinka extermination camp. The OSI predecessor, the Special Litigation Unit of the INS, investigated both suspects. It sent photographs of Demjanjuk, taken from his 1951 visa application, and of Fedorenko to the Israeli police. The police, in turn, included them in a photo spread presented to Holocaust survivors. The Fedorenko and Demjanjuk photographs clearly stood out from the rest in clarity and size, and the Israeli police found a witness who identified Demjanjuk as the sadistic Treblinka gas-chamber operator known as "Ivan the Terrible." Meanwhile, the Soviets provided OSI with a copy of an ID card from a German guard training facility at Travniki. The card appeared to have been issued in Demjanjuk's name in 1942. It carried his photograph, but the Soviets gave no information on the history of the card which, in any case, did not refer to Treblinka. The signature on the card seemed different from Demjanjuk's handwriting, and in fact, the card would later prove to be a forgery. When Allan Ryan saw the card, however, his reaction was, "You son of a bitch... We've got you."[11]

Realizing that the testimony of the Israeli witnesses might not be enough to achieve their goal, OSI lawyers interviewed a German named Horn who had served at Treblinka. Horn lived in Berlin and could not be subpoenaed, so his testimony was videotaped in the presence of Demjanjuk's lawyer. In the video-tape, Horn was presented with two photo spreads, one with the Travniki ID photo and the second with the 1951 visa application photo. Horn identified Demjanjuk as Ivan the Terrible from both photos. The Horn testimony, which confirmed the identification of Demjanjuk by the Israeli witnesses, convinced the trial judge in Demjanjuk's denaturalization proceedings that he was indeed Ivan the Terrible, and he was stripped of his citizenship in June of 1981.

At this point, Demjanjuk's lawyer learned that OSI had received information from the Soviet Union and Poland that was possibly relevant to his client. He requested the information be turned over to him. In denying the request, OSI attorney Bruce Einhorn asserted that "all relevant and discoverable documents in the government's possession" were already part of the record of the denaturalization proceedings, and that based on those documents Demjanjuk had lost his citizenship.[12]

After the U.S. Court of Appeals rejected his appeal, Demjanjuk was extradited to Israel in February 1986. There he was placed in a maximum-security jail cell and tried for the atrocities he allegedly committed at Treblinka, the second case of its kind since the conviction and execution of Eichmann in 1962. No one doubted that Demjanjuk faced the same fate. The defense attorney found expert witnesses to demonstrate that the Israeli police had used defective photo-identification procedures. The unreliability of those procedures raised serious doubts about Demjanjuk's identity, but the court ruled that he was guilty and, in 1988, sentenced him to death.

Death sentences in Israel are subject to mandatory appeal to the Israeli Supreme Court. During the course of the appeal process, the Soviet Union collapsed. In 1991, Demjanjuk's Israeli lawyer, Yoran Sheftel, managed to uncover evidence in Soviet judicial files, previously accessible only to government agencies, which demonstrated beyond a shadow of a doubt that "Ivan the Terrible" had been another Ukrainian by the name of Ivan Marchenko. Not until 1993, though, was Demjanjuk finally acquitted and allowed to return to his home in Cleveland.

Demjanjuk's defenders in the U.S. had always suspected that OSI was withholding evidence pointing to his innocence. In 1985, they discovered by chance that OSI agents regularly disposed of their trash in the garbage cans of the McDonalds's restaurant opposite the OSI offices on K Street. Monitoring the disposals, they found two reports of OSI investigators who had interviewed the witness Horn months before the videotape deposition shown at the trial. The report revealed that Horn had been unable to identify Demjanjuk from the first photo spread containing the 1942 photo, and that he had identified Demjanjuk from the second photo spread while Demjanjuk's first photo was left conspicuously within his sight. The reports would have enabled the defense to challenge the reliability of Horn's testimony.

Other "garbage-can" documents led to even more sensational evidence of an OSI cover-up: OSI files, since the beginning of the proceedings against Demjanjuk, contained one hundred pages of Soviet interrogations of former Treblinka guards, including statements identifying Marchenko as "Ivan the Terrible." These would lead to Demjanjuk's acquittal in Israel.[13]

Chief Judge Merritt of the U.S. Court of Appeals for the Sixth Circuit learned about these disclosures through the newspapers. Disturbed by the possibility that his court may have unwittingly sent an innocent man to face a death penalty, he reopened the Demjanjuk case in 1992 to determine whether OSI prosecutors had improperly withheld vital information from the courts and the defendant. On November 17, 1993, the court ruled that OSI had engaged in prosecutorial misconduct by failing to disclose the evidence in their possession indicating that Demjanjuk was not Ivan the Terrible. Describing the OSI behavior as "fraud on the court," the judges found that the government's obligation to work for justice had been disregarded and that outside pressures from Congress and Jewish organizations had fostered a win-at-any-cost attitude at OSI. The court concluded by vacating the judgments against Demjanjuk.[14]

Allan Ryan, interviewed by the *Huntsville* (Alabama) *Times* in 1991, spoke frankly about the handling of the Demjanjuk case: "It was one of the first cases we tried, and we were much on the line. If we had lost the case, we probably would have had a very short lifespan." As Demjanjuk's attorney put it, OSI was willing to shorten Demjanjuk's life to lengthen its own.[15]

OSI was not the only villain in this story. The Soviet and Polish authorities knew perfectly well that Demjanjuk was not Ivan the Terrible, even at the time his well-publicized trial in Israel began in 1986. Still, they did not come forward with the evidence that would have saved him from the gallows. Did the Israeli prosecutors also know about such evidence? There is no firm proof, but it is possible that their American counterparts would have passed on the information in view of their close cooperation throughout the Demjanjuk proceedings.

Perhaps the most remarkable aspect of this story is the total lack of remorse on the part of the members of the Justice Department. OSI tried unsuccessfully to prevent Demjanjuk from returning to the United States after his release in Israel[16] and is attempting to deport him a second time, alleging that even if he was not Treblinka's Ivan the Terrible, he may have served as a guard somewhere else. That Demjanjuk was subjected to thirteen years of prosecution, that he spent seven years in a maximum-security jail in Israel, and that he was sentenced to death by an Israeli court, all because of prosecutorial misconduct by OSI, has not affected the collective conscience of the Justice Department or that of Attorney General Janet Reno. She announced, without the slightest hint of contrition, that the goal of her department continued to be Demjanjuk's expulsion from the United States.[17] In this, she had the support of *The New York Times*, which called for a new trial "in justice to Mr. Demjanjuk,"[18] and certain Jewish groups. Rabbi Marvin Hier of the Simon Wiesenthal Center in Los

Angeles, for instance, described the court ruling authorizing Demjanjuk's return to the U.S. as a terrible decision and "misplaced compassion."[19]

As director of OSI during Demjanjuk's denaturalization trial, Allan Ryan would have been aware of the concealment of the evidence of Demjanjuk's innocence. Nevertheless, he was able to write this in *Quiet Neighbors:*

I came to realize that, as much as I loathed John Demjanjuk, I resented him more, with his impassive silence, his callous, almost bored, demeanor as he faced his accusers, his careless and demonstrably false alibi... He was cheating us, and much more than us, he was cheating history by his utter refusal to acknowledge his past. His guilt could not be disputed by any objective observer...yet Demjanjuk sat there, day after day, showing nothing.[20]

Curiously, Ryan did not refer in his book to a case involving a former German V-2 rocket expert, even though it was investigated during his term in office and involved a prominent defendant. Prosecution was delayed until after Ryan had left OSI; perhaps the tactics his lawyers proposed went beyond what Ryan was prepared to condone.

3. The Rudolph Case[21]

While studying at Harvard Law School, Eli Rosenbaum came across a book about the World War II Dora-Nordhausen underground factory complex in central Germany which included the manufacturing facility for the German V-2 rockets. Forced laborers worked in the complex, often under appalling conditions. Rosenbaum read that Arthur Rudolph, the manufacturing director of the V-2 plant, was part of a group of German rocket experts who were recruited after the war to work on the U.S. missile and space program at Huntsville, Alabama. When Rosenbaum joined OSI after graduating from law school in 1980, he persuaded his superiors to open an investigation of Rudolph.[22]

Prior to Rudolph's arrival in the United States in 1947, the American authorities thoroughly investigated his background. Rudolph admitted that he had been a nominal member of the Nazi Party, and that forced labor was used at the V-2 plant, but the investigation did not show that Rudolph personally mistreated the workers in his factory or engaged in other criminal actions. He became a U.S. citizen and played a leading role in the development of the NASA Saturn V rocket until his retirement in 1969.

In September 1982, the OSI contacted Rudolph, by then seventy-six years old, and requested him to attend a meeting during which he would be interrogated regarding his World War II activities. He had never heard of OSI, but having nothing to hide, he readily agreed. Allan Ryan, his deputy Neal Sher, and Eli Rosenbaum questioned Rudolph for five hours about his wartime activities, repeating in essence the inquiries of the U.S. Army investigators in 1947. They didn't explain the reason for the interrogation, saying only that questions had been raised about those activities. At the end of the meeting, Ryan cordially thanked Rudolph for being open and cooperative. In February 1983, OSI asked him to attend a second interrogation, this time conducted by Sher and Rosenbaum only. The questioning was a repetition of the previous meeting, except that Rosenbaum tried unsuccessfully to make Rudolph admit that he approved of the racial policies of the Nazis. Rudolph became worried and decided to consult a lawyer.

Rudolph heard nothing further from OSI for almost six months. During that period, Allan Ryan resigned from OSI and Neal Sher became acting director. On July 25, 1983, Sher wrote to Rudolph demanding to meet with his lawyer. The meeting took place in September. Sher and Rosenbaum told the lawyer that OSI would institute denaturalization and deportation proceedings against his client due to his role in the slave labor system at Dora-Nordhausen. They added that they would base their case on Rudolph's statements during the two interrogations, as well as a mass of evidence from witnesses whose names they were not prepared to reveal. The prospect of lengthy court proceedings, as well as the threat of possible loss of retirement benefits, upset the ailing, seventy-seven year-old Rudolph. OSI offered to drop the case if Rudolph would agree voluntarily to leave the U.S. and renounce his citizenship. After much agonizing, he accepted the offer and returned to Germany.

The OSI deal with Rudolph created a minor diplomatic incident. The German government did not appreciate being saddled with a stateless person considered a war criminal by the U.S. authorities. The German Embassy in Washington protested to the State Department and demanded that OSI hand over its file on Rudolph. After repeated demands over a period of nine months, Sher finally complied. The German authorities conducted their own investigation of Rudolph's wartime activities, and the reasons for OSI's reluctance to turn over the file soon became apparent. A German prosecutor contacted the nine Israeli and U.S. witnesses whose names were listed in the OSI file and discovered that four knew nothing about Rudolph, two were mentally unfit to testify, two gave evidence against Rudolph that was not credible, and one would have testified in favor of Rudolph. He found no grounds for prosecuting Rudolph, who was then granted German citizenship.

OSI had perpetrated a hoax that deceived both Rudolph and his lawyer who had no previous experience in Nazi deportation cases. OSI could not have brought deportation proceedings against Rudolph unless he was first denaturalized. But to strip him of his citizenship, OSI would have had to prove that he had obtained it through concealment or misrepresentation, an impossible task in that Rudolph had given a full account of his background prior to being admitted to the United States. Moreover, OSI falsely claimed to have reliable evidence against Rudolph in the hope of inducing him to give up his citizenship.

Rudolph subsequently brought suit in Federal Court in California to overturn the agreement with OSI on grounds of fraud. The government invoked the defense of sovereign immunity from suit by foreign nationals, and the case was dismissed.[23] OSI had indeed covered all the angles.

The Walus, Demjanjuk, and Rudolph cases illustrate a pattern of behavior by the Justice Department Nazi hunters: dependence on unreliable witnesses, concealment of evidence favorable to defendants, and a seeming indifference to justice. Such procedures may not have been standard for OSI, but with a chance of catching a "big fish," its attorneys adopted the "win at any cost" attitude. The Court of Appeals in the Demjanjuk case found this attitude to be inconsistent with the government's obligation to work for justice.

Kurt Waldheim was clearly a "big fish." Sher described the case as the most important in OSI's history. The Austrian was facing the Sher-Rosenbaum team. The only question that remained was whether he would fare any better than Rudolph.

CHAPTER III

The U.S. Government Intervenes

At the end of March 1986, OSI's reputation was at a high point, after all, OSI had recently succeeded in expelling John Demjanjuk, "Ivan the Terrible," from the United States to face trial in Israel. Eli Rosenbaum's letter to the attorney general requesting that Waldheim be placed on the Watch List was passed to OSI.

Except for a few right-wing critics such as Patrick Buchanan, no one had reason to doubt that OSI, as a part of the Justice Department's prestigious Criminal Division, operated in a strictly professional manner. Neil Sher had succeeded Allan Ryan as director of OSI, and although Rosenbaum had moved to the WJC, he and Sher remained close friends and mutual admirers. Rosenbaum, in fact, continued to refer to Sher as "Chief."

In the early pages of *Betrayal*, Rosenbaum described the encounter with Sher in Jerusalem in January 1986 during which Sher encouraged Rosenbaum to pursue the Waldheim investigation: "I could guess [Sher's] line of reasoning: Nobody likes Waldheim. So if there is any substance to this 'Nazi' charge, the chance to verify it and make it public was a war-crimes prosecutor's fantasy... 'Anything is possible,' Sher repeated. 'Especially with a fox like Waldheim.'"[1]

More than a year would elapse before Attorney General Meese acted on the WJC request. Meese's office had indicated at an early stage that no decision would be made prior to the Austrian elections. The U.S. government obviously did not want to be accused of interference. If the matter had been solely in the hands of OSI, Waldheim would have been included on the Watch List barely two weeks after receipt of the WJC request of March 25. On April 7, Sher addressed a memo to his immediate superior, Deputy Assistant Attorney General Mark Richard, asserting that solely on the basis of documents the WJC provided, sufficient grounds existed for excluding Waldheim from the U.S.[2]

Sher's memorandum unquestioningly accepted the WJC interpretations of the documents. Obviously written in great haste, the memo inaccurately described Waldheim as a counterintelligence officer. Sher then stated, "The fact that he was listed as a war criminal wanted for murder makes a compelling case for his being placed on the Watch List." Sher admitted in his memo that inscribing a person on the UN War Crimes Commission list did not constitute proof of the commission of war crimes. He also admitted that he made no inquiry into the background for Waldheim's listing; yet he found that listing a "compelling" reason for excluding him from the U.S. Sher did not explain, however, how the alleged war crime—the murder of deserters from the German Army—could trigger action under the Holtzman Amendment. This amendment addressed only persecutions based on race, religion, national origin, or political opinion.

Sher issued a second memo on April 21, 1986, which concluded with a clear recommendation: "Waldheim's name should be entered on the INS Watch List as an alien excludable from entry into the United States under 8 USC Section 212a33 [the Holtzman Amendment]." Again, Sher relied primarily on the UN War Crimes file, although he noted the possibility that it may have been politically motivated. He repeated that Waldheim's name on the UNWCC list was "more than ample basis" for placing him on the INS Watch List. Sher's memorandum was leaked to *The New York Times*. The *Times* quoted extracts in an article published on April 25, 1986, citing "a former Justice Department official" as its source. The article noted that Sher's superiors, and in particular the attorney general, had not approved the recommendation as it did not represent department policy. In Austria, the incident was viewed as part of the electioneering of WJC against Waldheim. Indeed, one must wonder whether the "the former Justice Department official" cited by the *Times* could have been Rosenbaum himself.

Waldheim recognized the seriousness of the threatened Watch List action, and he immediately took steps to head it off. He sent his son Gerhard, a Viennese banker, to Washington to defend him at an April 22, hearing on the Waldheim affair staged by the House of Representatives Subcommittee on Human Rights and International Organizations. Gerhard's arguments fell on deaf ears. Worse, he had to endure a vituperative attack on his father by Congressman Tom Lantos of California, a Holocaust survivor, who called Waldheim a "shameless liar" for denying knowledge of the Salonika deportations.[3]

Waldheim and the Austrian government also understood the need for the advice and assistance of an American lawyer. The Austrian Embassy asked Judge William P. Clark, who had held several high-level positions in the Reagan administration, for a recommendation. He proposed Donald Santarelli, a prominent Washington attorney.

A lean, tough Italian-American with a wry sense of humor, Santarelli knew the Justice Department well, having served there in a senior capacity during the Nixon and Ford administrations. He was on a first-name basis with Meese and his immediate subordinates. Clark led Santarelli to believe that if Waldheim's defense were conducted in a low-key manner, with as little publicity as possible, Meese would decide not to place Waldheim on the Watch List.[4]

Santarelli's first move was to request Sher's boss, Mark Richard, to authorize the submission to OSI of memoranda and other materials in defense of Waldheim as a matter of fairness and due process. Richard refused, stating that aliens in Holtzman Amendment cases were not entitled to due process.

Outraged, Santarelli contacted Meese and threatened to disclose Richard's position to the press. Meese thereupon instructed Richard and OSI to go along with Santarelli's request. Even so, Santarelli had few illusions about OSI's attitude toward Waldheim. He learned, for instance, that on a wall in the OSI reception room was a large reproduction of the now notorious photograph of Waldheim at Podgorica inscribed with the word "WANTED." Santarelli wrote to Meese to protest this display of undergraduate-style partisanship but received no reply.[5]

Between June and December 1986, Santarelli's office, with Gerhard Waldheim assisting, submitted to OSI a series of memoranda with supporting documentation[6] to address the Justice Department's areas of concern regarding Waldheim. These "areas," which Assistant Attorney General Stephen Trott had set forth in a letter to Santarelli, simply reflected the WJC accusations. There was, however, one addition: Trott indicated that the Department was interested in reviewing Waldheim's doctoral thesis without an explanation of how the thesis could be relevant to the allegations of persecution.[7] The Justice Department did not ask for clarifications or amplifications of the data supplied on behalf of Waldheim.

By the end of 1986, one of the main pillars of the anti-Waldheim campaign, the Yugoslav and UN war-crime charges, had collapsed. The Yugoslav government agreed in November to open up its files on the case, and Austrian government representatives, an OSI team (Neal Sher and historian Patrick J. Treanor), and Professor Herzstein, among others, inspected them.[8]

Herzstein described his findings in his 1988 book on Waldheim. In 1948, Waldheim was serving as an aide to Austrian Foreign Minister Karl Gruber who was then engaged in sensitive negotiations with the Yugoslavs over disputed territory in southern Austria. The Yugoslavs were aware that the young Austrian diplomat had served on General Loehr's staff, and they decided to manufacture bogus war-crime charges against him in an effort to embarrass Gruber. By the time the charges found their way into the UN war-crimes files, Waldheim had been transferred to the Austrian Embassy in Paris. The Yugoslavs did not drop their "bombshell," and the politically motivated accusations against Waldheim languished thereafter in the Yugoslav and UN archives.

Meanwhile, Sher continued to urge his superiors to place Waldheim on the Watch List,[9] but 1986 came to an end without a decision from Meese who has never publicly explained the reasons for the delay.[10] Most likely Meese was reluctant to go along with the OSI recommendation because of the harm it would do to U.S.-Austrian relations, and, one would hope, because of his doubts regarding the soundness of the OSI position. Moreover, President Reagan had declared in July 1986 that he had not seen any conclusive evidence of Waldheim's guilt and that consequently the U.S. should hold its fire.[11] According to Rosenbaum, this remark caused a panic at the WJC, and Steinberg decided to stir up the pot by issuing "fresh" evidence to the press, supposedly implicating Waldheim in the deportation of Jews from Greek Islands. Steinberg knew that the material had previously been published and did not refer to Waldheim, but, as Rosenbaum noted, his gambit worked. The press responded as anticipated and turned up the heat on Meese through repeated inquiries on the status of the Watch List investigation.[12]

Clearly, the Waldheim case was a hot potato. New York members of Congress, including Senator Daniel Patrick Moynihan and Representative Charles Schumer, had pressed the Republican administration to ban Waldheim as soon as possible. Jewish organizations, in particular the Los Angeles-based Simon Wiesenthal Center led by Rabbis Marvin Hier and Abraham Cooper, applied similar pressure.[13] Although their organization bore the name of the famed Austrian Nazi hunter, Cooper and Hier did not share Wiesenthal's cautious approach to the Waldheim affair. On the contrary, they were convinced of Waldheim's guilt and supported the Watch List action quickly and vociferously. Indeed, they sponsored a mammoth write-in campaign to this end. More than a million cards were given out carrying a reproduction of the Podgorica photo and the slogan, "America says no to Waldheim!" Hier claimed that the White House admitted to receiving the remarkable total of one hundred thousand cards.[14]

On March 5, 1987, The New York Times reported that Meese was likely to "undergo a grilling" by Representative Charles Schumer, a Democrat from Brooklyn, when Meese appeared on that date before the House Judiciary Committee to review his department's budget.[15] Schumer, representing a heavily

Jewish district, apparently was upset because Meese had failed to act quickly in the Waldheim case as well as in other Nazi war-criminal matters.

In early April, *The Washington Post*, citing "government sources," reported that OSI had renewed its recommendation to ban Waldheim in a 200-page memorandum. The sources claimed that "the evidence [against Waldheim] is so overwhelming that it meets a dozen times over" the Watch List legal requirements. The Post also quoted Allan Ryan, the former OSI director, as saying that the attorney general had not acted forthrightly in this case by failing to make a decision.[16]

According to Waldheim, in early 1987 Edgar Bronfman met with Meese and Secretary of State Shultz and complained that the administration was not adequately rewarding Jewish organizations for their political support. Bronfman allegedly decided that the position of these organizations during the 1988 elections would depend on the Republicans' attitude toward them, and that the administration could send a useful signal by placing Waldheim on the Watch List.[17]

On April 9, 1987, OSI submitted its "final" report to the attorney general. It concluded that Waldheim had engaged in persecutorial actions within the meaning of the Holtzman amendment. A copy was sent to Abraham Sofaer, the State Department legal advisor and a proponent of a Watch List decision.[18] Surprisingly, Secretary of State George Shultz, despite his responsibility for conducting U.S. foreign affairs, did not oppose the OSI recommendation, which was bound to sour relations with Austria.[19] Richard Schifter, the assistant secretary of state for Human Rights, tried to persuade Shultz that the evidence did not justify putting Waldheim on the Watch List, but Shultz did not want to listen. Sofaer had apparently convinced him that OSI had a good case, and that was the end of the matter as far as he was concerned.[20]

The Austrian ambassador in Washington during that period, Thomas Klestil, had previously served as Austrian consul general in Los Angeles in the 1970's. There he became a friend of Reagan and several future members of the Reagan administration, including Meese whose wife is German. Taking advantage of these personal relationships, Klestil fought hard to avoid the Watch List action, and for a while he was optimistic. He believed that Reagan and Meese would oppose it, and he hoped their opposition would be enough to counter the growing political pressure. In early April, however, one of Klestil's friends in the Administration warned him that such action was inevitable. The friend suggested that, since Klestil's term as ambassador was scheduled to end in early May, he might want to speed up his departure from Washington so as not to be in office when the Watch List announcement came out, signalling the failure of his efforts. Klestil, however, remained at his post to the end and continued his efforts on behalf of his chief of state.

On April 27, Klestil paid his official farewell call on President Reagan. Rumor has it that Reagan put his arm around Klestil's shoulder and said, "I am so sorry!" Klestil did not realize that Reagan was referring not to his departure, but rather to Meese's announcement to the press a few hours earlier in Brussels of the Watch List action against Waldheim.[21] Meese, with a straight face, had expressed the hope that the excellent relationship between the United States and Austria would not be affected by this decision which would brand the Austrian president as an agent of Nazi persecution.[22] In a separate press conference in Washington, a Justice Department spokesman announced that, in accordance with a department policy of not making internal investigative reports public, the evidence behind the decision would not be released.

This policy did not deter an "anonymous Justice Department prosecutor" from declaring to the press that on the basis of such evidence, he "would feel comfortable about the chances of getting a conviction against [Waldheim] as a war criminal under the Nuremberg trial rules."[23] The reticent prosecutor was no doubt Neal Sher who would express the same view to Austrian officials in May 1987.

The United States government had thus conferred its official blessing on the WJC accusations and provided a confirmation of Waldheim's guilt. On April 28, the Austrian government issued a statement protesting the Watch List action, declaring, "The administrative procedure applied is inexplicable and incomprehensible to the Austrian people and the Austrian federal government." The statement added that the government would take all steps necessary to protect the head of the state, and that the Austrian ambassador had been recalled for consultation. Some weeks later, in a *note verbale* to the Department of State, the Austrian Embassy declared that the Watch List action was unacceptable and stated:

> It must be stressed that the Austrian Federal President was democratically elected by the people, and according to the Austrian Federal Constitution, represents the Republic internationally. The decision of the U.S. Attorney General clearly affects the integrity of the Federal President and thus has a

vital political dimension for Austria and its role in the world. Austria would have assumed that the U.S. government would in the present context let considerations of foreign policy prevail over other political considerations.[24]

The Austrians were obviously convinced that the action against Waldheim was the result of domestic political pressures. According to Hans Reichmann, an Austrian diplomat, Chancellor Franz Vranitzky had been astounded to hear from Meese during a visit that the Reagan Administration had no complaints against Waldheim, had no proof of any wrongdoing on his part, had not investigated the archives relating to the Austrian president, and had only reacted as the result of a constituent, namely the WJC.[25] The Austrians were incensed by what they considered to be the unjustified withholding by the U.S. authorities of the evidence OSI claimed to have. The Justice Department's ostensible reason in not disclosing the Waldheim file was to avoid revealing its hand in case Waldheim were to challenge the OSI findings through litigation. In truth, he could only do so by attempting to enter the United States and subjecting himself to deportation proceedings, an inconceivable move on the part of a chief of state. The Justice Department concerns about disclosure were thus theoretical, and the Austrians suspected that they served to hide the lack of substance of OSI's case against Waldheim.

The State Department, no doubt worried about the foreign policy implications of the Watch List action, seemed willing to make concessions to defuse the crisis. According to Austrian Foreign Minister Alois Mock, a U.S. diplomat in Vienna assured him shortly after the Watch List decision that there was no obstacle to providing the Austrian government with the Waldheim documentation.[26] The U.S. government agreed to send a delegation to Vienna to explain the Justice Department's decision, and, as the Austrians had been led to expect, to turn over the documents. Mark Richard and Neil Sher, representing the Justice Department, together with Mary Mochary, deputy legal advisor of the Department of State, and Ronald Lauder, the U.S. Ambassador to Austria, met in Vienna on May 15, 1987 with Austrian government representatives headed by Thomas Klestil.[27]

Austrian Justice Minister Egmont Foregger opened the meeting, noting that the U.S. Department of Justice, at the request of the Austrian government, had agreed to disclose the documentary basis for the Watch List decision. He thanked the Americans for their cooperation and left the meeting. Ambassador Lauder then referred to the discussions as a "continuing dialogue, more worthwhile than a turnover of documents." In other words, the Austrians would not, after all, receive the promised evidence. Klestil angrily told the Americans that this situation was unacceptable because the public interpreted the Watch List action as a guilty verdict. He emphasized that the Austrian government expected facts and unambiguous proof.

Mochary explained that the Waldheim decision was a matter of internal American law, which the Justice Department had to enforce, and that the American delegation was not prepared to discuss facts. Sher and Richard referred to the Holtzman Amendment and OSI's jurisdiction, citing the Demjanjuk case as an example of bringing war criminals to justice. Klestil interrupted to point out that President Waldheim was hardly in the same category as Demjanjuk. At this point, Mochary stated that the United States could not be held responsible for the world's view of the Waldheim case. This was a curious statement. In fact, the portrait of Waldheim as a Nazi and a war criminal was largely due to the press releases the WJC fed to the American mass media.

The Austrians repeated their demand that the parties discuss the facts behind the Waldheim case and proposed that the Americans meet with the Austrian experts who had investigated the Yugoslav war-crime files in Belgrade and had concluded that they were not credible. The Americans refused, and the discussions temporarily broke down.

When the meeting resumed, Mark Richard described the six accusations of persecution contained in the OSI brief without offering any back-up materials. Richard conceded there was doubt about the reliability of the Yugoslav-UN war-crime file, thus revealing why the Americans did not want to discuss the subject with the Austrian experts. Richard declared that the Watch List decision was irreversible, and the American delegation had not come to Vienna to reopen the investigation. Klestil repeated that the American position was unacceptable to the Austrian government.

Ambassador Lauder, who evidently did not believe in presumption of innocence, then made the following remark for which he was severely criticized in the Austrian press: "How is it possible for this man not to be guilty, after being accused of fifteen or sixteen misdeeds?"[28] Lauder, who hailed from a wealthy New York Jewish family, had already made himself unpopular in Vienna by conspicuously refusing to attend President Waldheim's inauguration.[29]

As the meeting ended, Sher declared that in his opinion the available evidence was sufficient to secure a conviction of Waldheim as a war criminal under the Nuremberg rules. Mochary hastened to add that this was only Sher's personal opinion.

Thus the Austrians were given no satisfaction. On the contrary, Sher's remarks on Waldheim's probable criminal liability simply turned the knife in the wound and made the refusal to turn over the evidence even more of an affront to the Austrians. They were in effect told to mind their own business. The Watch List decision was a matter of internal U.S. law, and the damage to Austria's interests was not the U.S. government's concern. Even less of its concern was the personal harm inflicted on Waldheim. He had lived for almost fifteen years in the United States, where he had made many friends. He was now being cut off from a significant part of his past.

The Watch List decision was a devastating blow for Austria and Waldheim. The U.S. government had more or less branded him a war criminal, and even though it refused to reveal the basis for the condemnation, the general public would be inclined to accept a finding from such a high-level source. The Austrian government obviously wanted to clear Waldheim's name and restore the prestige of the Austrian presidency, but since the Americans refused to disclose their evidence, how could this be done? A task force consisting of former Foreign Minister Karl Gruber and two members of the Austrian Foreign Affairs Ministry—Dr. Ralph Scheide and Dr. Ferdinand Trauttmansdorff—prepared a documented rebuttal of the accusations against Waldheim based primarily on the materials that had been submitted to the U.S. Department of Justice on Waldheim's behalf. Still, the Austrians realized they needed more drastic action to achieve their goal.

In 1986, Simon Wiesenthal had suggested to Waldheim that the charges against him should be examined by a committee of independent military historians, but Waldheim, while not opposed to the idea, believed it would involve serious logistical and organizational problems.[30] The Watch List action, however, called for urgent countermeasures, and on May 7, Waldheim requested Chancellor Franz Vranitzky to appoint a commission of historians as Wiesenthal had suggested.[31] Waldheim argued that the commission's findings would surely absolve him and that if its members had recognized expertise and independence, would also offset the effects of the Watch List decision, perhaps inducing the U.S. government to reconsider.

Vranitzky, a Socialist politician, had replaced Sinowatz as Chancellor following Waldheim's election. No friend of Waldheim, he nevertheless attempted, unsuccessfully, to have the Watch List action rescinded during an official visit to Washington on May 21, 1987.[32] Vranitzky readily agreed to implement Waldheim's proposal, assigning the responsibility to the Foreign Ministry. No one foresaw that a supposedly independent group of historians would prove unable to remain above the politics and emotions which the Waldheim affair generated.

CHAPTER IV

The International Commission of Historians

In the late afternoon of February 8, 1988, the six members of the International Commission of Historians headed for the Chancellery on the Ballhausplatz to deliver their report on the five-month investigation of Lieutenant Waldheim's World War II military service in the Balkans. Representatives of the media were present in force, as rumors had been circulating that the document would not please the Austrian government and President Waldheim.

After passing through an array of television cameras, klieg lights, and photographers, the commissioners were ushered into the chancellor's office, where the Swiss chairman, Hans Rudolph Kurz, formally handed over copies of the report to Chancellor Vranitzky and Foreign Minister Alois Mock. Kurz, accompanied only by the American and Belgian members (the others having refused to go along), then proceeded across the street to the ornate presidential office in the Hofburg Palace and delivered another copy to the man whose past they had been investigating.[1]

Waldheim received the historians courteously, even though he had learned that the report's conclusions would reflect negatively on him. Ill at ease, Kurz said to Waldheim: "Mr. President, you are not going to like what we are giving you. It will be hard to swallow, like bad stewed fruit (*ein schlechtes Kompott*)."[2] Kurz's quaint phrase accurately characterized the report, and Waldheim's composure turned out to be justified. In fact, while the body of the report representing the historical analysis of Waldheim's military service contained no evidence of any wrongdoing on his part, the unfavorable conclusions of the historians appeared to contradict the results of their own research.

That a team of supposedly professional and impartial historians would deliberately disregard their own findings of fact may seem unbelievable, were it not for the context of the anti-Waldheim campaign. The Austrians were convinced, when they set up the Commission, that a review of the allegations against President Waldheim by historians would confirm his denials of any wrongdoing.

They were right, but they had not foreseen the possibility that some members might not be impartial, and that consequently the Commission would become another arena for attacking the Austrian president.

This unexpected development was, ironically, a consequence of the Austrian government's determination to ensure the Commission's complete independence and thus avoid the appearance of a whitewash. To achieve this goal, Chancellor Vranitzky decided that the government would appoint a chairman who would be given a completely free hand in choosing the other five commissioners. In the interests of impartiality, the Austrian Ministry of Foreign affairs, responsible for establishing the Commission, chose a Swiss as chairman: Hans Rudolph Kurz, a retired Swiss civil servant and former head of the Swiss Army Historical Service. The choice turned out to be unfortunate. Kurz was suffering from a painful and debilitating hip disease, which seriously affected his mobility and his capacity as chairman to influence and direct the work of the Commission.[3]

On July 4, 1987 Kurz was officially appointed chairman of an International Commission of Historians whose assigned mission was to determine "whether there was personal culpable behavior on the part of Dr. Waldheim during his military service." Although the Austrian government would finance the Commission's expenses, the Foreign Ministry assured Kurz that he could freely choose the other members and that there would be no interference with the work of the historians. Kurz named the following persons to the Commission:

- Brigadier General (ret.) James Lawton Collins Jr. (USA), former head of the U.S. Army Center of Military History. Kurz thought that it was important to have an American member, because much of the documentation regarding the Waldheim affair was located in the United States. Collins, who had participated in the campaign against Germany following the Normandy invasion, had no preconceived views on the Waldheim affair, but his limited knowledge of German inhibited his contributions to the investigation.
- Gerald Fleming (United Kingdom), reader emeritus at University of Surrey. A German Jew who had moved to England and acquired British nationality, Fleming was the author of a book on the Holocaust and had specialized in the history of World War II. He had previously assisted the WJC in its research on Waldheim.[4] He was the only historian to solicit Kurz for membership on the Commission.[5]
- Professor Manfred Messerschmidt (Germany), director of the West German Military Archives in Freiburg. Because of his expertise on German Army matters, Messerschmidt was probably the most influential member

of the Commission. He soon displayed an anti-Waldheim bias, possibly because he was a Socialist and perhaps also because, as a German, he was not unhappy to see a prominent Austrian involved in a war-crime scandal.[6]

- Dr. Jean Vanwelkenhuyzen (Belgium), former head of the International Committee of World War II History. Kurz chose him because he wanted another neutral member on the commission. Vanwelkenhuyzen was unbiased, and he performed his mission with the open mind of a professional historian.

- Professor Yehuda Wallach (Israel), Professor of military history at Tel Aviv University. Waldheim had been accused of participating in the deportation of Greek Jews, so Kurz thought it advisable to include an Israeli historian. Wallach would echo the views of his government regarding Waldheim. Vociferous and aggressive, Wallach acted more as prosecutor than historian.[7]

Kurz considered appointing the leading Austrian military historian, Manfried Rauchensteiner, but abandoned the idea when Wallach threatened to resign, claiming that such an appointment would jeopardize the Commission's independence.[8] Professor Hagen Fleischer of the University of Crete, who had previously declared that Waldheim had not been involved in deportations of Jews from Greece, was named as special advisor to the Commission on matters involving Greece.

The Commission began its work in Vienna in September 1987 in spacious, high-ceilinged offices in the Pallfy Palace that the Foreign Ministry made available along with a secretarial staff. During this month, the Austrian government published its rebuttal of the accusations against Waldheim. Entitled *Kurt Waldheim's Wartime Years—A Documentation*,[9] the 300 page book consisting mainly of documents came to be known as the "White Book." Although the WJC and OSI promptly branded it the "Whitewash Book," it served as an important source of information for the historians, and General Collins described it as an "excellent study."[10] The "White Book, " which contained a detailed chronology of Lieutenant Waldheim's military service in the Balkans, showed that he had held the following assignments:[11]

(1) April-May 1942 – liaison officer with the Italian Pusteria infantry division in Montenegro which was engaged in anti-partisan activities.
(2) June-August 1942 – junior supply officer in a German-Croatian task force engaged in dislodging Yugoslav partisans from the Kozara Mountains in

Bosnia.

(3) September-November 1942 – staff interpreter with Army High Command 12 in Arsakli, Greece, in the neighborhood of Salonika.

(December 1942-March 1943 – study leave in Vienna)

(4) April-July 1943 – member of German liaison staff at Italian Army headquarters in Tirana, Albania, serving as interpreter.

(5) July-October 1943 – junior staff officer on German liaison staff attached to the Italian Army command in Athens, Greece.

(6) October 1943-April 1945 – adjutant (03) with the intelligence staff of Army Group E (successor to Army High Command 12) at Arsakli until October 1944, and then at various locations in Yugoslavia as the German Army retreated. During this period, he was on home leave for nearly four months, completing his doctoral thesis and getting married.

(7) April 1945 – assigned to a German infantry division in the Trieste area, but the war ended before he was able to reach his new unit.

This information, derived from Waldheim's army records and uncontested by his accusers, showed that, far from being a key figure in the German Balkan army, Waldheim had served in minor staff positions without command authority. It also revealed that he had been granted extensive home leaves which permitted him to complete his law studies.

With documentary support the White Book also rebutted the WJC accusations against Waldheim concerning:

• Membership in Nazi organizations
• Involvement in the deportation of civilians to concentration camps
• Involvement in the planning of anti-partisan operations
• Involvement in the deportation of Italian prisoners to Germany
• Involvement in the deportation of Jews from Salonika and from Greek Islands
• Dissemination of anti-Semitic propaganda pamphlets (the historians did not consider this charge worth investigating)
• Involvement in the illegal execution of captured English commandos
• Ordering retaliatory executions in Yugoslavia (the Yugoslav and UN warcrimes files)

Thus, much groundwork for the Commission's task had already been done through the publication of the White Book. The historians were given copies of the numerous press releases and reports published by the WJC, but the WJC refused to grant the Commission access to its files on Waldheim and publicly branded the historians as tools of the Austrian government.[12] Rosenbaum, unable to shed his inquisitorial role, criticized the Commission's failure to appoint a prosecutor or attorney to its staff or to insist that Waldheim testify under oath.[13]

The Commission was aware that OSI, in connection with the Watch List decision, had investigated Waldheim's Balkan years and therefore might have some valuable information in its files. General Collins was assigned the task of obtaining access to them. As Collins later put it, OSI was absolutely no help. Neal Sher wrote to Collins stating that OSI would gladly release its files if Waldheim legally challenged his exclusion from the U.S. by applying for a visa. This response greatly annoyed Collins as it was obvious Waldheim would never do such a thing.[14] OSI shared WJC's negative views on the Commission. According to press reports, an OSI lawyer described the Commission as "a farce" and the historians as not serious about their work.[15]

By the end of January 1988, the historians, after having checked relevant archives in Germany, Austria, Italy, Greece, and Yugoslavia, realized that further investigations were not likely to turn up new information regarding Waldheim, and they began drafting their report. Their work was briefly interrupted when the German weekly *Der Spiegel* published a document it had purchased for 50,000 Deutsche Marks from a Yugoslav historian, Dusan Plenca, indicating that Waldheim had been personally involved in sending Yugoslav civilians to concentration camps.[16] The document represented the first time a "smoking gun" had surfaced, but it soon proved to be a crude forgery, and the magazine apologized to Waldheim.[17]

In the final stages of their work, the historians asked Waldheim if he would be willing to be interviewed in order to clarify certain matters involving his Balkan service. Waldheim readily agreed, and the Commission proposed to send him an advance list of the points to be covered. Word of the proposal somehow reached OSI, for the Commission received a telex from an Associated Press correspondent in Vienna who claimed to be transmitting a message from the U.S. Justice Department. The message demanded that the questionnaire be withdrawn, or else the Commission would be accused of misconduct. General Collins told the reporter that if the U.S. government had any comments on the Commission's activities, it should transmit them through official channels.

Shortly thereafter, the Associated Press correspondent telephoned the Commission's Austrian secretary, insisting that the matter was serious and that the commission would be in trouble if it did not comply with the Justice

Department request.[18] The historians decided to ignore this attempt at blackmail, and articles soon appeared in the press criticizing the decision to give Waldheim advance notice of the Commission's questions.

The historians interrogated Waldheim at his home for four hours on January 26, 1988, but they learned nothing new as Waldheim asserted that many of the subjects were outside the scope of his knowledge. The transcript of the meeting shows that the historians had difficulty finding relevant questions to discuss with Waldheim.[19]

The Commission's report, dated February 8, 1988, consisted of 212 typewritten pages in the German language.[20] Following an introduction describing the Commission and its work methods, the report began with a short chapter on Waldheim's attitude toward National Socialism, including his doctoral dissertation and his alleged membership in Nazi organizations. Here the Commission seems to have gone beyond its mandate from the Austrian Foreign Ministry which was limited to an investigation of allegations of misbehavior during Waldheim's military service.[21] The report concluded that there was no indication that Waldheim had any commitment to Nazi ideology and cited specific evidence of his anti-Nazi views.

The next section, which Messerschmidt drafted, discussed the history of the German Army in the Balkans and, by way of background, described in general terms the reprisal measures against the partisans without any reference to Waldheim's possible participation. It then covered the organization and functions of the intelligence staff of Army Group E. Its description of the division of tasks and functions between the intelligence and counterintelligence sections supported Waldheim's assertions that he was not involved in, nor informed about, the counterintelligence activities which included liaison with SD (Security Service) and other security units. The report pointed out that the intelligence staff did not issue orders regarding reprisal activities. These were the responsibility of the combat units, and the report confirmed that as an 03 officer Waldheim had no command or decision-making authority. His main function, the report noted, was to collate and analyze reports from subordinate units and prepare daily and monthly enemy-situation reports. The WJC had alleged that "special assignments," one of the organizational duties of an 03 officer, meant that Waldheim could have been involved in "liquidation" actions, but Messerschmidt stated that in the Wehrmacht the term did not have the same sinister connotation often attributed to its use in the context of the SS or SD.[22]

The report continued with a discussion (drafted by Fleming) of the treatment of captured British commandos, who, under Hitler's "commando order," were subject to execution if engaged in sabotage operations. Noting that Waldheim was not involved in their interrogations, the report found that as part of his job of preparing daily intelligence bulletins he had initialed a number of documents that referred to commandos. Yet it cited no document implicating Waldheim in the turn over of captured commandos to the SD for execution. The report claimed, however, that through the initialing of the documents, Waldheim was part of the prisoner "handling process," but it did not explain how his "involvement" could have influenced the fate of the commandos.[23]

Wallach drafted the next section, dealing with the deportation of Jews from Greece, with a pronounced anti-Waldheim bias and a disregard for the facts. The historians had been unable to find any evidence of Waldheim's participation in the deportations, and so Wallach concentrated on demonstrating that Waldheim had lied in denying any knowledge of these events. This issue seemed to obsess Wallach. He dwelt on it at length during the Commission's interview of Waldheim,[24] but he failed to prove his case. The only document Wallach cited was a field report to the German liaison staff in Athens indicating that the Jewish Committee in the Greek city of Ioannina was a possible center for an "uprising."[25] Waldheim's initials appeared on a copy of this report to attest to the authenticity of the copy (*"fuer die Richtigkeit der Abschrift"*). This Wallach misinterpreted to mean a certification to the accuracy of content, implying knowledge. Wallach also argued that Waldheim's signature on the document proved that there was no strict division of tasks between the intelligence (Ic) and counterintelligence (AO) functions—a gross error on Wallach's part, for at that point Waldheim was not serving as an intelligence officer.[26] Moreover, Wallach's argument contradicted Messerschmidt's earlier conclusion that the Ic and AO functions were kept separate.[27] General Collins had no doubts concerning the Commission findings. He declared in a speech in 1990 that "it was pretty definite from the investigations that [Waldheim] had nothing to do with the evacuation of Jews."[28]

Next, the report dealt with the removal of Italian soldiers from Greece to labor camps in Germany following Italy's surrender. At that time, Waldheim was still a member of a small German liaison staff in Athens that handled negotiations with the Italian army command. Although the WJC had accused him of participating in the deportation of the Italians, the historians produced no evidence of Waldheim's involvement in, or even knowledge of, this matter.

The last major topic the historians covered related to a number of anti-partisan campaigns. In their closing remarks on the *Kampfgruppe Bader* (the Pusteria division) and Operation Schwarz (the Podgorica meeting) matters, they specifically acknowledged the lack of evidence of Waldheim's participation in wrongful acts involving partisans and even the unlikelihood of such participation. Concerning the Kozara operation, in which Waldheim served as a junior supply officer, they concluded that "it was highly probable that [Waldheim] was not involved in the 'sifting' procedures used to select prisoners and refugees in the Croatian camps." This had been the principal WJC accusation.[29] The historians had no trouble in disposing of the allegation that the award of the Croatian *Zvonimir* medal to Waldheim proved that he had rendered exceptional services in combat against the partisans. They agreed with Waldheim that the medal had no special significance. It had been awarded to a large number of German army personnel including non-combatants, such as chaplains and paymasters.

The report reviewed in detail the WJC allegations relating to the destruction of several villages in the Stip-Kocane area by troops under the command of Captain Egberts-Hilker. The historians found no evidence linking Waldheim to the Stip-Kocane massacres. They rejected the contention of the WJC that Waldheim's enemy-situation report was a causal factor and declared that the Yugoslav Resolution (*Odluka*) that accused Waldheim of war crimes was mistaken in attempting to involve Waldheim in this and other incidents.[30]

The last topic in the report involved a number of reprisal actions of the German Army against Greek villages. The historians cited no evidence linking Waldheim to the massacres, and they noted that in several cases he was in Vienna when the atrocities took place.

The final chapter, entitled "Concluding Remarks," was the only part of the report that received any significant publicity. The historians first described their mission in the following irreproachable language:

> The Commission saw its task as attempting to determine the historical facts in as objective and comprehensive a manner as possible and to arrive at an assessment, without any preconceived opinion or predetermined direction, of the role played by Waldheim in the theaters of war in which he was active. This task was to be carried out according to methods of historical inquiry, based on all accessible sources, in particular the official documents and papers it was still possible to locate and consult. The Commission views itself as a purely scholarly and scientific body of enquiry. It has no judgmental function. Its task is solely and exclusively to present the facts as they appear to the Commission on the basis of the available sources. It remains the prerogative of those who ordered the report and the recipient of the

report to draw whatever appears to them to be the necessary conclusions.

Unfortunately, the historians did not abide by these sensible guidelines. They proceeded to cite four instances where "Waldheim had duties which *may* (emphasis added) have affected the fate of prisoners or refugees."

- The transmission of interrogation reports on commandos, which the historians found to be "causally connected with their subsequent fate." No explanation of such causality appeared in the body of the report.
- In Western Bosnia, Waldheim "was in the immediate proximity of criminal acts," but the historians admitted they found no evidence of Waldheim's direct involvement.
- In Athens, Waldheim "was aware of the practice of transporting Italian prisoners/internees to Germany." The relevant section cited no evidence that Waldheim had been thus aware, much less involved. The historians added that as the 01 staff officer, Waldheim "probably had only limited practical possibilities of influencing the course of such events." They hedged their opinion with the word "probably," even though it should have been obvious that a staff lieutenant would have had *no* opportunity to influence such a major policy decision.
- In Arsakli, Waldheim's role as intelligence officer in charge of reporting on the enemy situation could be characterized in the same manner, namely knowledge of certain events, but also "probably" limited possibilities of influence.

Notably absent from this enumeration is any reference to the deportation of Jews. The historians summarized their findings as follows: "The picture that emerges is one of differing *proximity*, depending on position, to measures, and orders that were incriminating in terms of the laws of war." Although proximity to criminal acts has never been considered proof of guilt, the historians again hedged by stating that "these conclusions do not provide a final answer to the question of Waldheim's wartime guilt."

Not having found any evidence of Waldheim's personal involvement in criminal actions, as a "scientific body of inquiry" the historians should have so concluded and stopped there. Instead, they invoked a theory of guilt by knowledge and proximity: "In general terms, even the mere knowledge of infringement of human rights near one's place of duty may constitute a certain guilt—if a person, for lack of strength or courage, disregarded a human duty to intervene." To support their intimation of Waldheim's possible guilt, the historians declared that Waldheim was "undoubtedly far more than just a junior-level desk officer in his staff function" without, however, giving any explanation for this opinion. The report then declared:

> The Commission has not noted a single instance in which Waldheim protested or took steps—to prevent, or at least to impede its execution - against an order to commit a wrong that he must doubtlessly have recognized as such. On the contrary, he repeatedly assisted in connection with unlawful actions and thereby facilitated their execution.

This remarkable paragraph, often cited by Waldheim's enemies, calls for several comments. First, the historians overlooked the fact that Waldheim, as a young lieutenant in an admittedly non-executive staff function, would not have been a recipient of unlawful orders and therefore could not have been in a position to prevent or impede them. Secondly, there is no basis at all in the substantive part of the report for the assertion that Waldheim "repeatedly assisted in connection with unlawful actions and thereby facilitated their execution." If indeed the historians had found evidence to that effect their conclusion regarding Waldheim's guilt should have been clear.

Having virtually rendered a guilty verdict, the historians softened the blow:

> One circumstance in Waldheim's favor is the fact that he had only extremely modest possibilities of any sort of opposition to the wrongs being committed. The practical possibilities for counteraction were very limited for a young member of staff who had no power of command at the level of the army group. In all probability, such actions would not have led to any concrete result.

The "circumstance in Waldheim's favor" effectively demolished the historians' theory of Waldheim's possible guilt by knowledge and proximity. Nonetheless, in the final paragraph of the report, the historians once again condemn Waldheim:

> Waldheim's own description of his military past does not tally at many points with the findings of the Commission. He attempted to let his military past slip into oblivion, and when that no longer proved possible, to play it down and make it appear innocuous. His lapses of memory are, in the view of the Commission, so basic that it was not able to obtain any elucidating indications from Waldheim for its work.

Neither the report nor the minutes of the meeting between the historians and Waldheim justify such a highly negative epilogue. The historians were apparently echoing the "cover-up" charges made against Waldheim, but the issue was certainly outside the scope of their mission and not covered by the report, which does not identify any basic "lapses of memory."

Waldheim and the Austrian government, not surprisingly, were outraged by the conclusions of the report. Despite the lack of any evidence of Waldheim's guilt, it appeared to support his accusers. The report had indeed turned out to be the mess that Kurz had announced.

The question that must be asked is how this came about. And the answer is clear. The Commission's work was compromised from the beginning. Three of the Commission's members—Wallach, Fleming, and Messerschmidt—far from being the unbiased scholars the Austrians had expected Kurz to appoint, appeared determined to condemn Waldheim. Their hostility toward the Austrian President was such that they refused to accompany the other commissioners when they submitted a courtesy copy of the report to Waldheim. Six years later, Messerschmidt would use distorted excerpts from the transcript of the meeting between Waldheim and the historians to prove that Waldheim had been evasive in his answers.[31]

The original wording of the concluding remarks and final paragraph, as drafted by Messerschmidt, was even harder on Waldheim:

The Commission thinks that Waldheim knew that he shared a responsibility in the events discussed. But, after the war, he did not have the strength of character to admit this. On the contrary, he tried to cause his military past to be forgotten. His efforts to pass over in silence certain periods of his life, his not always believable inability to recall certain events, and his manner of hiding behind obedience to orders evidence his unwillingness to recognize his undeniable share of moral responsibility.

The Austrian government learned about the text and called on Kurz to delete the reference to "moral responsibility." Kurz, prepared to refuse, viewed the request an infringement of the Commission's promised independence, but in the meantime, the neutral commissioners, Collins and Vanwelkenhuyzen, also objected to the proposed wording, which even Wallach and Fleming were not prepared to defend. Messerschmidt was obliged to redraft the concluding para-graph. Despite the deletion of the reference to "moral responsibility," this paragraph was only marginally more favorable to Waldheim.[32]

Having failed in their effort to brand Waldheim as morally responsible for German crimes in the Balkans, the anti-Waldheim commissioners nevertheless succeeded in surreptitiously modifying the report to Waldheim's detriment. Vanwelkenhuyzen had been responsible for the section of the report dealing with Waldheim's student days and his alleged Nazi affiliations. In the text he submitted in French to the Commission's secretariat for translation and inclusion in the final report, Vanwelkenhuyzen concluded that Waldheim had not been a Nazi and that there was no indication that he ever intended to join the Nazi party. This conclusion evidently did not please one or more of Vanwelkenhuyzen's colleagues. Two days after his return to Brussels, he received a telephone call from a member of Waldheim's staff expressing surprise that he had attributed to Waldheim the intention of joining the Nazi party. Vanwelkenhuyzen denied having written anything of the sort, but the caller insisted that the report so stated. After checking his copy, Vanwelkenhuyzen realized with astonishment that his text had been "improved" to state the opposite of what he had written without his having been asked or informed. He told the Austrians that he stood by his original wording.[33] Messerschmidt, primarily responsible for putting the report together in its final German version, was the person in the best position to modify the Belgian's text. He has denied any responsibility for this piece of dishonesty.

The result of the Commission's work was a poorly drafted document prepared by a committee dominated by persons not wholly devoted to producing an unbiased historical analysis. Wallach, Fleming, and Messerschmidt, unable to prove that Waldheim had been involved in German war crimes, were unwilling to close the report on a note favorable to him. They therefore insisted on including the negative comments that appeared in the concluding remarks.

Despite their misgivings, the neutral Belgian and American members, having succeeded in deleting the reference to moral responsibility, were unprepared to provoke another fight. They had to deal with opinionated and domineering colleagues who were fluent in the governing German language. Wallach, a big man with a loud voice, would express preemptory judgments while pounding the table with his fists. Fleming, who specialized in long-winded speeches, supported Wallach, and in a quieter fashion, so did Messerschmidt. This formidable trio managed to control the Commission proceedings, brushing aside the ailing Swiss chairman. Although Kurz did not necessarily agree with the anti-Waldheim commissioners, he was unable to stand up to them.[34]

Ironically, the WJC and OSI, which from the beginning had been scornfully critical of the Commission, hailed the report as a confirmation of their allegations against Waldheim.[35] The WJC and OSI undoubtedly were well informed of developments within the Commission. Rosenbaum recounts in his book that shortly after the historians interrogated Waldheim, he received a "confidential" telephone account of the meeting.[36] The report's allegation that Waldheim had "repeatedly assisted in connection with unlawful actions" sounded like language justifying a Watch List decision. Was it only coincidence?

The ambiguous conclusions of the historians led to renewed calls for Waldheim's resignation and did not silence Waldheim's critics. However, the conclusions could not hide the fact that the Commission had been unable to find a single piece of evidence linking Waldheim to culpable behavior, despite the determination of some of its members to find it. Waldheim announced to the media that the historians had vindicated him, provoking an angry reaction from Wallach, with Messerschmidt supporting him, at a Commission press conference held the day after the release of the report. Wallach accused Waldheim and the Austrian press of misinterpreting the Commission's findings, despite Kurz's statement that the Commission had found no proof of Waldheim's guilt.[37] To anyone who took the trouble of reading the historians' report, though, it was clear that the Commission itself had misinterpreted its own work.

In the meantime, a British television company launched its own investigation of Waldheim's wartime years in preparation for the production of a televised "trial" of the Waldheim affair. Waldheim, suspecting another media attempt to depict him as a war criminal, reacted at first with hostility. The results would, however, please him greatly.

CHAPTER V

The Thames Television "Trial"

On July 15, 1987, a tall, bearded Englishman by the name of Jack Saltman flew to Vienna to meet President Waldheim. Saltman was a television program executive at Thames Television, a leading British television corporation, and he had been put in charge of producing a televised "trial" of Kurt Waldheim based on the WJC charges. HBO, a U.S. cable company, developed the concept and brought in Thames Television to produce the program at about the same time the Austrian government was establishing the International Commission of Historians. Although the goals of the two projects were the same—to inquire whether there was any basis for the accusations against Waldheim—HBO and Thames intended to test the evidence in the adversarial context of a simulated judicial proceeding. The producers believed that the drama of a trial was particularly suitable for television and only in such a context could the Waldheim affair be definitively elucidated.

Saltman, who recorded the history of the production in a book entitled *Kurt Waldheim—A Case to Answer?*,[1] had come to Vienna to brief Waldheim on the background and purpose of the program and to solicit his help and cooperation. He knew that Waldheim, as chief of state, would never agree to participate in person. But he also knew that Waldheim's staff had accumulated a great deal of information on his wartime years, and Saltman hoped to tap that source. Saltman did not expect a warm reception. The media outside of Austria, and especially in the United States, had been hard on Waldheim who no doubt would be expecting more of the same from Thames Television. Moreover, being the "defendant" in a television "trial" was bound to be a humiliating prospect for the Austrian chief of state.

Waldheim received Saltman with his customary politeness, but he did not hide his hostility toward the proposed program. Waldheim viewed it, as Saltman had expected, as part of the continuing media campaign against him. Saltman explained that the Thames program would be different. It would permit an impartial and dispassionate examination of the accusations which surely could only be to Waldheim's advantage. Waldheim closed the short meeting by saying, "If you were to search for a hundred years, Mr. Saltman, you will find no evidence that will reveal me as a war criminal."

Despite Waldheim's antagonism, his personal assistant, Dr. Ralph Scheide, sensed some good might come out of the Thames program, and he promised Saltman that requests for information would be honored.[2]

In preparing for the project and hoping to obtain access to their Waldheim files, Saltman visited the WJC and OSI during a trip to the U.S. in November 1987. At the WJC, Saltman once again was faced with suspicion and hostility, but for different reasons.[3] He was received by the WJC executive director Elan Steinberg and Beate Klarsfeld, an aggressive, high-*profile* Nazi hunter based in Paris. WJC leaders were bitterly opposed to the idea of a television "trial" of Waldheim and hoped that the presence of the formidable Klarsfeld might help persuade Saltman to drop the project. Klarsfeld had led several anti-Waldheim demonstrations in Austria during the presidential campaign. At his inauguration, she unfurled a banner with the legend, "No To The War Criminal President."[4] As a true believer in Waldheim's guilt, she was a valued ally of the WJC.

Klarsfeld and Steinberg told Saltman they were totally against the program. Steinberg expressed the fear that no television program would do justice to the evidence. Saltman replied that his concern was to get the evidence to do justice, but to no avail, as Steinberg refused to commit himself to providing any data for the program. Saltman suspected the WJC had been overstating its case against Waldheim, which would explain why it was trying to discourage an open and impartial examination of the evidence. Then too, if the television trial were to absolve Waldheim, the WJC could always claim that the result would have been different had its evidence been produced.

Saltman ran into another stone wall when he visited OSI director Neal Sher a few days later. Sher refused to make the OSI files available to Thames. At the same time he asserted that his safe contained a report, complete with 262 footnotes, representing "conclusive proof of Waldheim's culpability." Echoing WJC views, Sher told Saltman the television "trial" was a stupid idea, and Thames would be better off producing a documentary on the Waldheim affair.[5]

Undeterred by the negative attitudes of the WJC and the OSI, Saltman concentrated on putting the program together. After consulting a number of judges and lawyers, he concluded that the idea of staging a full-fledged trial, complete with a jury, would be inappropriate in the absence of a defendant. He chose, therefore, to structure the program as a commission of inquiry, which would examine the evidence and decide whether there was a case for Waldheim to answer, much like a U.S. grand jury proceeding. The commission would consist of five professional judges. A "presenting" counsel would submit the case against Waldheim, and a "challenging" counsel would defend him.

Finding a competent and motivated prosecutor to act as presenting counsel would be crucial to the success of the program. Saltman's first choice was a prominent American trial lawyer, Gerry Spence, who had previously appeared as defense counsel in a televised "trial" of Lee Harvey Oswald. Spence had planted the idea of a Waldheim television trial at HBO, expressing an interest in the role of prosecutor. After studying the available evidence against Waldheim, Spence began to have serious doubts that he could persuade a panel of judges that there was indeed a case for Waldheim to answer,[6] and he backed out.

Saltman turned to the former director of OSI, Allan Ryan, who was working on the legal staff of Harvard University. Ryan enthusiastically agreed to act as "presenting counsel." Echoing Neal Sher, he told Saltman that if he were the prosecutor in a real trial, he was sure that he could secure a conviction against Waldheim for war crimes.[7] Still imbued with Nazi-hunting zeal, Ryan viewed the prospect of obtaining a verdict against Waldheim, if only in a mock television trial, with great satisfaction. He seemed to be an ideal choice for the role.

Saltman had an easier time finding the defense, or "challenging," counsel. Lord Rawlinson of Ewell, one of Britain's leading Queen's Counsel, had served as attorney general in the Heath government in the 70's and had represented Thames Television in a recent court proceeding. When Saltman asked him to undertake Waldheim's defense in the program, he agreed, after being assured that Thames would spare no effort in researching Waldheim's Balkan career.

Given Rawlinson's impeccable credentials and reputation, his participation in the program made the task of filling in the panel of commissioners considerably easier. Saltman was able to recruit the following five distinguished former judges:

- Sir Frederick Lawton, a retired English judge who had served for many years on the Court of Appeal; he would act as Chairman
- Gustav Petren, a former member of the Swedish Supreme Administrative Court
- Shirley Hufstedler, a former U.S. Circuit Court of Appeals judge and Secretary of Education under President Carter
- A. Gordon Cooper, a former judge of the Appeal Division of the Supreme Court of Nova Scotia, Canada
- Walter Huebner, a former judge of the Federal High Court of Appeal,

Stuttgart, Germany

They were to proceed under the following terms of reference: "Whether this Commission—restricting their consideration solely to statements, documents, and submissions presented at the hearing—are of the opinion that there is enough evidence to warrant an answer by Dr. Kurt Waldheim to allegations that he wrongly participated in acts which were contrary to the international laws of war."[8]

To support the program, Saltman organized an investigation of the allegations against Waldheim. This investigation would be far more comprehensive than the inquiries of the International Commission of Historians. Allan Ryan estimated that the amounts Thames expended on its research exceeded the resources the U.S. government could be expected to devote to investigating Waldheim. Saltman described the Thames research program as follows:

For the previous five months, we'd had journalists and/or academics working for us in West and East Germany, Austria, Greece, Israel, Italy, Britain, the United States, Canada, Yugoslavia, Norway, Sweden, South Africa, Poland, Switzerland, Albania, Bulgaria, France, and Ireland—a total of nineteen countries. They'd interviewed over 250 people, locating thirteen of Kurt Waldheim's wartime colleagues who had never before spoken in public. They visited twenty-nine archives in more than a dozen countries, and had retrieved over 1000 separate documents, some of which had not seen the light of day since they had first been filed.[9]

The files the Thames program generated were subsequently donated to the Institute of German, Austrian, and Swiss Affairs at the University of Nottingham, England.[10]

The research failed to produce a "smoking gun." On the contrary, it demonstrated that some of the accusations against Waldheim were so lacking in proof that Ryan decided not to present them to the commission of inquiry. The weak allegations included Waldheim's participation in Operation Schwartz (the famous Podgorica photo), the dissemination of propaganda leaflets (the historians had also discarded this charge), and the Stip-Kocane reprisal actions (with the related Yugoslav and UN war crime files)[11.]

The charges Ryan considered worth pursuing were 1) Kampfgruppe Bader – massacre and deportation of prisoners; 2) Kampfgruppe West Bosnia (Kozara) – massacre and deportation of prisoners; 3) Athens – killing of Greek civilians and deportation of Italian prisoners; 4) Arsakli – deportation of Jews from Greek Islands and execution of captured British commandos.

The proceedings before the commission of inquiry were recorded at the Thames studios in Teddington, an attractive riverside village west of London. The filming lasted nearly fifty hours due to the many witnesses who had to be examined and cross-examined. These included Lt. Col. Bruno Willers, Waldheim's commanding officer in Athens, and Lt. Poliza, who served with Waldheim on the intelligence staff of Army Group E. Unable to produce evidence implicating Waldheim in the alleged crimes, Ryan tried to make a case based on Waldheim's knowledge of and proximity to criminal acts.[12]

Rawlinson, in his closing statement, compared the Waldheim affair to a lynching party. Referring to his experience as Britain's former chief prosecutor, Rawlinson declared, "On this evidence, no court would convict, no committal would be made by a magistrates' court, or, I would suggest, a grand jury. No law officer would launch a prosecution."[13]

On June 5, 1988, the program, called "Waldheim: A Commission of Inquiry" appeared on U.S. and British television and was seen in a number of other countries as well. The fifty hours of tape had been condensed to three and a half hours of broadcasting time. To prevent leaks to the press and to preserve the suspense of the program, the verdict was broadcast live at the end of the program. The chairman, Sir Frederick Lawton, read the five-page opinion in which the commissioners unanimously concluded that "the evidence which has been put before us is not enough to make it probable that Lt. Waldheim committed any of the war crimes alleged against him in this inquiry." Reviewing the charges Ryan presented, Lawton noted that in each case no evidence had been introduced which showed that Waldheim had participated in any way in the commission of war crimes. Specifically rejecting the notion of guilt by knowledge or proximity, the commissioners declared:

Dr. Waldheim could only be guilty of [war crimes] if he would prove by evidence to have knowingly helped by some active involvement those who have in fact committed them. A person actively involved would include one who had a duty and a power to prevent a crime but who failed to intervene. A person does not commit a war crime merely because he knows that others have committed such crimes, nor because he worked with or alongside those who committed them. Suspicion is not knowledge; lapses and aberrations of memory, such as Dr. Waldheim feels to have had about his service in Greece and the Balkans, are not in themselves evidence of guilt.[14]

The Thames program was the only occasion when the historical records and witnesses relating to Waldheim's Balkan service were examined in an adversarial context corresponding as closely as possible to a court of law. As Lord Rawlinson subsequently attested, the program was prepared with a strict sense of fairness. A verdict against Waldheim would no doubt have helped the commercial success of the venture, but Saltman's book shows that the producers made no attempt to influence the outcome. Sir Frederick Lawton explained to the press prior to the recording of the "trial" why he had agreed to participate in the program. He said that the numerous allegations appearing in the press against Waldheim had been supported by few facts, disturbing his sense of fairness. Unless properly investigated, such allegations would, in his opinion, endanger historical accuracy. For this reason, he and his fellow commissioners had agreed to take part.[15]

Professor Telford Taylor, a former Nuremberg trial prosecutor who acted as consultant for the Thames program, added: "I see no reason to apologize for the fact that [the trial] is taking place on television. It's better to get a reasoned debate with jurists about the accumulated evidence than what we've been getting."[16]

OSI Director Neal Sher attacked the program in the press a few days before its broadcast. Sher, who had never had any qualms in calling Waldheim a war criminal while refusing to reveal the basis for the accusation, told *The New York Times*[17] that the idea of a television tribunal rendering a decision on the Waldheim case was not only preposterous, but also dangerous, unfair to Waldheim, and misleading to the public. He added: "We're secure enough in our [Watch List] decision not to care what the verdict is. My big concern goes beyond Waldheim. This kind of program demeans the serious efforts being made here and elsewhere to call to account those who engaged in Nazi crimes and persecution. You don't try a man on TV."

Former Congresswoman Elizabeth Holtzman echoed Sher's attack. She declared that she was terribly troubled by the television program, saying, "Nobody is accountable in that courtroom except to HBO."[18]

Elan Steinberg, of the WJC claimed that a show trial would trivialize the legitimate processes for dealing with suspected former Nazis and would threaten to create a distorted public record. Steinberg overlooked the fact that the record had already been distorted by his organization.[19]

Despite a verdict unambiguously in Waldheim's favor, the program did not materially improve Waldheim's public image in the U.S.. The preview tape HBO made available to the press did not include the decision of the judges, which was not yet known. The television critics could only speculate on the outcome of the "trial," but clearly they were not rooting for Waldheim. David Bianculli of *The New York Post* wrote, "A judicial Jimmy the Greek, after watching the HBO inquiry, would lay heavy odds on Waldheim's being found guilty on a majority of the counts."[20]

In a half-page article, John J. O'Connor, *The New York Times* reviewer, gave high marks to the program for "scrupulously adhering to the elevated formality of a high-level inquiry" and for avoiding even a hint of sensationalism. However, his description of the "trial" had a distinctly anti-Waldheim flavor. He said Allan Ryan, the prosecutor, "emits hints of profound moral outrage," while the defense counsel, "Saville Row natty" Lord Rawlinson, "hews closely to purely legalistic points." O'Connor claimed that the case for Waldheim was "decimated" by former "Nazi" military men (who were in fact Wehrmacht officers) rallying to the support of Waldheim with the "defiant retort: 'you can't prove it'" when confronted with implicating documents and "sheer common sense." O'Connor concluded dramatically, "At this point, the rest of us might want only to look away, profoundly repelled and as much in sorrow as anger." Evidently, O'Connor thought there *was* a case for Waldheim to answer. To prepare for the possibility that the judges would view the matter differently, O'Connor virtually eliminated their role by declaring that the tribunal's decision "is perhaps superfluous."[21]

In the same issue of the *Times*, an editorial praised the Thames-HBO program, stating it demonstrated the usefulness of "docu-trials." While admitting the hearing did not convict Waldheim of anything, the editorial could not resist a slap at Waldheim by finding, quite irrelevantly, "a devastating contrast" between the account of a surviving British prisoner's mistreatment by his German captors and "old soldiers who, like Waldheim, insisted they never took part in war crimes."[22] Readers who did not watch the program would probably remain unaware that the tribunal had unanimously absolved Waldheim. To learn the outcome, they would have had to spot a three-paragraph article by O'Conner buried in the television section of the *Times* the following day and repeated the day after. The article reported the verdict without commenting on the tribunal's conclusion.[23]

In a tribute to the seriousness of the Thames program, the British Ministry of Defence would use it extensively as a source in preparing its 1989 report on the involvement of Lt. Waldheim in the fate of captured British commandos, the last major inquiry into the Waldheim affair.

CHAPTER VI

The UK Ministry of Defence Investigation

In February of 1988, Greville Janner, a Labor Party Member of Parliament, rose in the House of Commons and called on the Thatcher government to investigate Kurt Waldheim's possible involvement in the criminal murder of British commandos captured by the German Army in Greece. Janner, a prominent English Jew (now Lord Janner), had close ties to the WJC and OSI. He had been a war-crimes investigator for the British Army and was the leader of a parliamentary group engaged in facilitating the prosecution of Nazi war criminals residing in the United Kingdom.[1]

Janner had first raised the Waldheim matter in Parliament in May of 1986. Hoping to enlist the aid of the British government, the WJC had initiated the process by providing Janner with copies of German Army documents. These indicated that Waldheim may have been involved in the processing of captured British commandos.[2] This possible involvement was, of course, a matter of great interest to the British government and public. The fate of seven British commandos captured by the Germans in 1944 remained unknown. There was, however, a strong presumption that German security forces had executed them. The Ministry of Defence was instructed to review its records, along with the WJC documents Janner furnished, to determine whether Waldheim had any criminal involvement.

At the time Waldheim was inaugurated as president in July 1986, the Ministry investigation had not been completed. Nevertheless, Janner protested Prime Minister Margaret Thatcher's sending of the customary message of congratulations to Waldheim and urged the government to ban him from entering the United Kingdom.[3] The prime minister refused to do so, stating that the British government had nothing against Waldheim. On August 1, 1986, the British foreign secretary, Sir Geoffrey Howe, wrote to Janner to inform him that "neither the Ministry of Defence's records nor the papers you have provided can be regarded as offering evidence of any criminal activity on the part of Lieutenant Waldheim concerning the fate of the commandos."[4]

The publication of the report of the International Commission of Historians in February 1988 provided Janner with an opportunity to reopen the Waldheim matter. The historians had stated, without explanation, that Waldheim's passing on of commando interrogation records was "causally related" to their execution by the SD, implying Waldheim's criminal responsibility.[5] The British government could not ignore such language, and Prime Minister Thatcher informed Janner that the results of the 1986 investigation be reviewed in light of the historians' report. She reminded the House of Commons that the government had taken "very seriously" the allegations concerning Waldheim's involvement with British servicemen but so far had found no basis for the allegations.[6]

A few days later, the minister of state for the Armed Forces notified Janner that the review would be as thorough and comprehensive as possible and that a report would be published upon its completion. Professor Sir Harry Hinsley, Master of St. John's College, Cambridge, would monitor it to ensure its objectivity and thoroughness.[7] Clearly, the British government was determined to lay the Waldheim matter to rest once and for all.

The Ministry of Defence review took a year and a half to complete and its findings were published by Her Majesty's Stationery Office in October 1989. The 115-page report was entitled, "Review of the results of investigations carried out by the Ministry of Defence in 1986 into the fate of British servicemen captured in Greece and the Greek Islands between October 1943 and October 1944 and the involvement, if any, of the then Lieutenant Waldheim." As sources, the Review listed documents made available from a number of national archives, particularly in the United States and Germany. It acknowledged the assistance of a number of organizations, such as Thames Television, OSI and the WJC. The Thames Television program and Saltman's book were extensively cited as sources in the Review. In a letter to the minister of state for the Armed Forces dated 5 July, 1989, Professor Hinsley confirmed that, in his opinion, the report had examined all available evidence on the subject in an objective manner.[8]

The documents produced by the WJC and reviewed by the historians and Thames Television related to three specific cases of captured commandos. The Ministry's Review, in its effort to be all encompassing, covered all other instances where British military personnel were captured by the Germans while Waldheim was stationed in Arsakli, but found no evidence of his involvement. The Ministry's Review even examined—and rejected—an improbable assertion by a former British serviceman that Waldheim had somehow been involved in the shooting of British prisoners of war in a camp in Italy in 1944. Waldheim had never served in Italy.

The accusations against Waldheim regarding British commandos were based either on their mistreatment or their transfer to the SD under Hitler's so-called Commando Order. This order called for the execution of enemy personnel captured while engaging in sabotage activities. The Review indicated that no evidence had come to light that Waldheim had been personally involved in interrogating prisoners or that he had been in any way responsible for the beating of prisoners that had allegedly taken place in Salonika jails.

The Review examined in detail three commando cases involving Hitler's order where documents showed some involvement or awareness by Waldheim, resulting in the WJC allegations:

(1) In the Cephalonia case, Waldheim's initial appeared on a report that implied that the captured commander of the commando party, Captain Warren, could have been involved in sabotage operations. The WJC and the historians assumed that Waldheim's remark concerning Warren caused him to be turned over to the SD for execution, but the Review noted that German troops had captured the Cephalonia party while Waldheim was on leave, and that German field-unit messages to headquarters had already labeled the commandos a "sabotage party." The Ministry therefore concluded that the report from Waldheim's office was not responsible for triggering the application of the Hitler order and Captain Warren's subsequent execution.

(2) In the Alimnia case, the commandos were also captured while Waldheim was on leave, and reports describing them as commandos subject to Hitler's order had already been sent to higher headquarters. The Ministry found no evidence of Waldheim's involvement in the transfer of the prisoners to the SD for execution. His initials appear only on a covering letter transmitting interrogation reports to the headquarters of Army Group E in Belgrade.

(3) In the Calino case, Waldheim's initials appear on an intelligence staff report. This report containing the statement that Sgt. Dryden, leader of the commando party, would be passed to the SD in accordance with the Hitler order. There was no evidence, however, that Waldheim initiated or authorized this statement. And as he lacked command authority, he

could not have been responsible for such action. Dryden was not turned over to the SD and he survived the war.

The director of Army Legal Services reviewed the Ministry of Defence's findings and concluded:

I have considered carefully both contents of the documents which were submitted and of this Review. At all material times, for the purposes of this Review, the then Lieutenant Waldheim was a mere junior staff officer. There is no evidence here, in my opinion, of relevant delegated executive authority or of any causative overt act or omission from which his guilt of a war crime may be inferred.[9]

The minister of state for the Armed Forces, Archie Hamilton, informed the House of Commons on October 17, 1989 that the government accepted the findings of the Review that, "No evidence has come to light to indicate that as a junior staff officer, [Lt. Waldheim] had the power either to order or to prevent [the fate of the commandos] or indeed to affect the outcome in any way."[10]

The British government, which had every incentive to seek out those responsible for the murder of British soldiers in World War II, thus unequivocally exonerated Waldheim from any responsibility for the fate of the commandos. No apologies, however, were forthcoming from the WJC or the OSI for having falsely accused Waldheim in this matter. On the contrary, Neil Sher, the director of OSI, told *The New York Times* on October 17, 1989, "To say that [Waldheim] had no involvement is preposterous, clearly absurd." But Sher did not justify his opinion. He added that the Review would have no effect on the Justice Department's decision to bar Waldheim from the United States.[11]

Elan Steinberg of the WJC declared, irrelevantly: "Kurt Waldheim's big lie that no British commandos were interrogated at his World War II German Army headquarters has finally been put to rest."[12]

During the period the British government was investigating the commando accusations, George Bush was elected president of the United States. Waldheim sent President Bush a private letter asking for his assistance in revoking the Watch List decision in light of the findings of the Commission of Historians and the Thames Television tribunal.[13] Waldheim knew Bush well since Bush had served as the U.S. Ambassador to the UN at the time Waldheim was Secretary

General. Bush did not reply, but six months later Waldheim received a letter from Bush's attorney general, Dick Thornburgh, thanking Waldheim for his letter on behalf of President Bush. Thornburgh wrote that the U.S. government not only considered the Watch List action to be "well founded in U.S. law," but also that a change in the decision would "not be in the best interests of U.S.-Austrian relations."[14] Despite the accumulating evidence of Waldheim's innocence, Washington would not budge on the Waldheim affair, as it continued to rely on the still secret and therefore unchallengeable OSI report. Still unanswered was the question of whether the report really contained, as Neal Sher repeatedly claimed, conclusive proof of Waldheim's guilt.

CHAPTER VII

The Release of the OSI Report

Edgar Bronfman Sr., the high-profile president of the WJC, had called on the international community to view the 1986 election of Waldheim as an act of symbolic amnesty for the Holocaust. At the same time, he declared that even though Waldheim would take office, it was not the end of the affair. He promised that "representatives of moral conscience" would continue to dig into Waldheim's past.[1] The Justice Department's decision to place Waldheim on the Watch List, in which the WJC had played a key role, ensured the success of a continued campaign against President Waldheim. This listing was the equivalent of a guilty verdict by the U.S. government, and few publicly doubted its good faith. In a visit to Brussels, Bronfman demanded that the European Commission not admit Austria into the European Union as long as Waldheim was that country's president.[2]

For the American public, subjected as it had been to more than a year of WJC allegations, there could no longer be any doubt that Waldheim was a Nazi war criminal. Those who dared disregard the American verdict by associating with him were subjected to vitriolic attacks, even blackmail. The most prominent victim was Pope John Paul II, who received Waldheim at the Vatican in 1987. Believing in the principle of presumption of innocence, the Vatican did not consider the unsupported Watch List decision as proof of guilt. The Pope's initiative raised a storm of protest from Jewish organizations.[3]

Rabbi Arthur Hertzberg, a professor of religion at Dartmouth College and a vice president of the WJC, referred to "burning outrage" among Jews. Perhaps fearing a libel action, Hertzberg cited only the fact that Waldheim had "looked away" while Jews were murdered as the source of this outrage. In truth, Waldheim's presence at such events had never been alleged.[4] Jewish organizations also bitterly attacked German Chancellor Helmut Kohl for having met with Waldheim in 1992.

The Watch List action provided an opportunity for an excursion into U.S. foreign affairs by eight members of the Foreign Affairs Committee of the House of Representatives, including Tom Lantos of California and Robert Torricelli (now senator) who represented a heavily Jewish district in New Jersey. Having learned that the Turkish prime minister Turgut Ozal had officially invited Waldheim to Ankara in November 1988, the congressmen dispatched a telegram to Ozal demanding that he cancel the proposed visit. In a thinly veiled threat they declared that the visit would have "a very negative effect" on Turkish-U.S. relations. They asserted, inaccurately, that the American people and the American Congress had expressed their view of Waldheim by banning him from even visiting the United States. Ozal did not cancel the Waldheim visit, but it was nevertheless downgraded to an unofficial stopover in Istanbul.[5]

Waldheim has claimed that State Department pressure induced several African heads of state to cancel his scheduled visits to their countries (Namibia, among others).[6] There is no doubt that by declaring Waldheim *persona non grata*, the U.S. government had seriously limited Waldheim's ability to represent his country abroad. Although the U.S. refusal to disclose the evidence against Waldheim seemed arbitrary and unjust, it was difficult to believe that the Americans would have acted against him without solid proof of his guilt. This proof, the Justice Department proclaimed, was laid out in the secret, jealously guarded, 204-page OSI report.

Still, there were a few skeptics. Henry Grunwald, the respected former editor of *Time* magazine, was one of the rare persons who was granted access to the report. He had been appointed U.S. ambassador to Austria in December 1987, following Ronald Lauder's resignation, and was shown a copy of the report at the State Department as part of his briefing process. He was struck by the polemical tone of the document and its repeated use of un-lawyerlike phrases such as "he must have" and "he probably did." However, Neal Sher assured him that the report provided ample basis for the Watch List action. Grunwald was instructed to be polite, but cold, toward President Waldheim, and Grunwald complied by looking grim-faced whenever he was photographed in Waldheim's presence.[7]

Bill Billet, the president of the U.S. Forces in Austria Veterans Association based in Red Lion, Pennsylvania, examined all available facts regarding Waldheim's World War II activities but found no evidence of war crimes or Nazi affiliations. In 1989 Billet and members of his association met with Waldheim in Vienna and appointed him an honorary member of their group. In 1992, Billet wrote to President Bush and urged the United States remove Waldheim from the Watch List. Olaf Grobel, director of the State Department's

Office of Central European Affairs, rejected the request in a letter to Billet stating that the Justice Department had "ample evidence" of Waldheim's involvement in persecutory activities. Grobel's letter said the Watch List action was "in no way directed at the office of the Austrian president, the Austrian people, or the Republic of Austria."

John Mapother, a retired CIA officer, was the most active Waldheim supporter in the United States. From the beginning, he had been skeptical about the existence of evidence the OSI claimed to have uncovered. Thoroughly familiar with the Austrian political scene, having served in Vienna in the early post-war years, he was an expert on German-speaking Europe. He continued to follow and write about developments in that area from his home in Potomac, Maryland. When the WJC launched its campaign against Waldheim in 1986, he found the allegations unbelievable, and he was appalled by what he considered to be the biased and superficial reporting of the matter in the American press.[8]

After the Watch List decision, Mapother decided it was time to act. He demanded access to the OSI file under the Freedom of Information Act and when his request was turned down, he sued the Justice Department to compel its release.[9] The Department vigorously opposed Mapother's suit, claiming that disclosure of the file would prejudice any subsequent enforcement proceedings involving Waldheim. The case languished in the courts for six years. More delays seemed inevitable, and ultimate success doubtful, had it not been for the publication of Eli Rosenbaum's book on the Waldheim affair in October 1993. Ironically, Rosenbaum, who rejoined OSI in 1988 and became its deputy director, provided the weapon that would force the Justice Department to disclose the Waldheim report.

Rosenbaum described in his book how OSI had secretly passed onto him parts of the Waldheim file for review in 1986 when he was still with the WJC.[10] David Vladeck, Mapother's attorney, recognized this as a golden opportunity to pressure the Justice Department into releasing the file. In December 1993, he sent devastating letters to the U.S. attorney in charge of the Mapother case and to a senior official in the Criminal Division, in which he pointed out that the publication of Rosenbaum's book had completely undermined the Justice Department's position under the Freedom of Information Act. How could the Department possibly justify withholding the Waldheim file from the public, Vladeck asked. Had not the deputy director of OSI disclosed in his book that he was given special access to OSI files while he was at the World Jewish Congress, at the same time acknowledging that no one outside the Justice Department was supposed to see the material? Vladeck pointed out that Rosenbaum's book was published five years after he had returned to OSI, raising the suspicion that the author made use of the still-secret OSI files on Waldheim. Rosenbaum's book made it abundantly clear, Vladeck wrote, that OSI and WJC had worked hand-in-hand in their campaign against Waldheim. This charge exposed OSI to more criticism, along the lines of the Demjanjuk case, that it was catering to the interests of Jewish groups instead of working for justice. Vladeck threatened to call on Rosenbaum to testify under oath on these matters. He concluded that, in his view, the legal issues the Justice Department raised in the Mapother case were a smokescreen to hide the Department's real concern, which was to ensure that OSI files in the Waldheim case not be exposed to public scrutiny.[11]

Undoubtedly the disclosure in court of Rosenbaum's role in the Waldheim investigation would have been acutely embarrassing to the Department and would surely have led the court to order the release of the OSI files. A decision to release the files was probably made soon after receipt of Vladeck's letters, as hints to this effect soon appeared in the press. On January 20, a Reuters dispatch quoted unidentified sources as saying that the Justice Department had recommended release of parts of the Waldheim file.[12] By early March, however, nothing had happened. The Justice Department was evidently faced with the agonizing decision: to release or not to release the files. Either alternative could lead to serious problems. On March 10, Vladeck filed a Notice of Deposition requiring Eli Rosenbaum to testify regarding his book on Waldheim.

The reaction was immediate—on March 11, Reuters reported that it had obtained excerpts of the "soon-to-be released" Waldheim Report.[13] Around 10:30 that evening, a senior OSI official called Vladeck and asked him if he planned to remain at home for the rest of the evening. To Vladeck's astonishment, an OSI representative rang his doorbell one hour later and handed him a copy of the OSI Report. Vladeck suspected that the Department apparently engaged in these strange after-hours activities to be able to claim that the Waldheim file had been turned over to the plaintiff the same day as its release to the press. In any event, it was clear that the press had been well briefed by OSI: *The New York Times*[14] and *The Washington Post*[15] carried stories in their March 13 Sunday editions that uncritically reflected the government's position.

The next morning, Saturday, an OSI messenger delivered another copy of the report to Mapother at his home, and a few days later OSI turned over hundreds of pages of background documents to Vladeck and Mapother, including internal OSI memoranda and the lengthy submissions of Waldheim's lawyers. The documents revealed, as Mapother had suspected, that OSI had not discovered any new evidence against Waldheim. It had relied almost entirely on documents the

WJC had provided. OSI stated in its report that it had not undertaken a full-scale investigation "as would normally be done in one of our cases," an extraordinary admission in a matter involving the chief of state of a friendly country.[16]

The OSI report on Waldheim, 204 pages long and dated April 9, 1987, had been issued under the following names: Neal Sher, director; Michael Wolf, deputy director; Patrick Treanor, historian; and Peter Black, supervisory historian. Twenty-six often gruesome photographs originating from Yugoslav archives and depicting concentration camps, prisoners, and scenes of shootings were attached as an appendix, but none had anything to do with Waldheim. The introduction stated:

> The factual analysis was undertaken by OSI's historical staff, which has earned a worldwide reputation among scholars and prosecutors in this field. As is evident in the report, facts and conclusions are fully documented and supported. Any suppositions or assumptions are identified as such and are based upon known German military procedure and practice. *Extreme care has been taken to be overly cautious* (emphasis added); we are fully confident of the reliability and accuracy of any assumptions or extrapolations. Indeed, we would have no hesitancy in relying upon them in a court of law.[17]

That Justice Department lawyers would not hesitate to rely on "assumptions" and "extrapolations," presumably in lieu of facts, in a court of law may seem strange, but in any event, "suppositions," "assumptions," and "extrapolations" predominated in the OSI report. Far from taking "extreme care...to be overly cautious," the report made no attempt to be even-handed, or to give Waldheim any benefit of a doubt.

Setting the stage for a review of the specific charges, OSI tried to demonstrate that Waldheim had more power and influence than might be expected from his rank and age. The report alleged he was "a very experienced junior officer, and it was a mark of the confidence his superiors had in him that he was chosen to extend that experience" in the Balkans.[18] On the contrary, Waldheim's assignments to staff positions after recovering from a wound that rendered him unfit for further combat duty seemed completely routine.

Attempting to build up the importance of "Ordonnanz Offizier," or "adjutant," Waldheim's function during his Balkan assignments, OSI incorrectly translated this term as "special missions staff officer," giving it an overblown and sinister ring.[19] OSI described such officers as occupying "responsible and very sensitive positions on the staff, one step below the general staff officers." Curiously, OSI also defined *Ordonnanz Offizier* as "essentially aides-de-camp or camp adjutants...junior officers who were attached to the senior staff officers."[20] OSI admitted that Waldheim did not have any command authority, [21] but failed to mention that he was granted unusually long leaves of absence to complete his law studies in Vienna, and that during the last two and a half years of the war, he was not promoted. These points would have undermined OSI's portrayal of Waldheim as a key staff officer.

Having thus pictured Waldheim as an important member of the Nazi war machine, the report went on to describe nine acts of alleged persecution, identical in all respects to the WJC accusations, which led to the Watch List action:

(1) Eastern Bosnia – Battle Group Bader. Charge: As member of a German liaison unit with the Italian Pusteria division, Waldheim participated in the transfer of the division's prisoners to slave labor camps.

Basis for the charge: an unsupported assumption that there could be "hardly a doubt"[23] that Waldheim, as a liaison officer, would have played a role in this transfer, citing no witnesses or supporting documents.

(2) Western Bosnia – Operation Kozara. Charge: While acting as deputy to the supply officer of the West Bosnia battle group, Waldheim was involved in acts of persecution against civilians, including Jews in Banja Luka, and partisan prisoners.

Basis for the charge: the possible involvement of the supply officer in the transfer of prisoners away from the battle zone, a perfectly legal activity, leading to the unsupported assumption based on phrases such as "it seems most likely" and "there can be no doubt"[24] that the supply officer and his deputy, Lt. Waldheim, were responsible for the subsequent execution of prisoners or their deportation to concentration camps. The OSI assertion that Waldheim was involved in the arrest and deportation of Banja Luka Jews in July 1942 was patently false. While admitting that the Croatian police were responsible for the round-up of the Jews, OSI cited a Croatian police document that referred to the deportation on August 7, 1942, of thirteen additional Jews, turned over to the police by German authorities. But, according to OSI's own chronology of Waldheim's service his unit had moved to another location forty miles from Banja Luka during the last days of July.[25]

(3) Operation Black – Montenegro. Charge: Waldheim's participation in a campaign against partisans during which atrocities were allegedly committed.

Basis for the charge: the famous photograph of Waldheim at a meeting of German and Italian commanders at Podgorica airfield, which he attended as an interpreter, as OSI admitted. Citing no evidence of any other Waldheim involvement in Operation Black, the report claimed that, simply because of his presence at the meeting, Waldheim "cannot be disassociated from this operation," that "he clearly participated and assisted in the operation," and that "his involvement was essential to the coordination of the operation." If Waldheim were "essential," it was only as an interpreter.[26]

(4) Athens – Summer-Fall 1943. Charge: As member of the German liaison staff attached to the Italian 11th Army, Waldheim was involved in reprisal operations carried out against Greek civilians by German units and in the deportation of Italian soldiers to slave-labor camps following Italy's surrender.

Basis for the charges: With regard to reprisals, the report referred only to Waldheim's war diary entry indicating that the German First Mountain Division was being informed of Hitler's order regarding the shooting of captured insurgents, and to Waldheim's signature, for authentication purposes, on a copy of a proposal from the First Mountain Division regarding deportation of civilians. Unable to explain how these items proved involvement by Waldheim in acts of persecution, the report could only state that Waldheim, "at the very least,"[27] was fully aware of the German anti-guerilla measures. On the Italian deportation issue, the report cited no evidence of Waldheim's involvement and did not allege that Waldheim had any authority to order the transfer of Italian prisoners to Germany.

(5) Army Group E – Arsakli. Charge: Waldheim's participation, as adjutant to the Intelligence Branch chief, in the deportation of Jews from Corfu and Rhodes in 1944.

Basis for the charge: None is apparent in the report. The report refers to "Lt. Waldheim's Ic/AO Branch"[28] providing intelligence data to a subordinate unit in Ioannina regarding the presence of 1,600 Jews on Corfu, implying that Waldheim was involved despite the fact that such intelligence data would have been within the jurisdiction of the counterintelligence (AO) section and not Waldheim's military intelligence (Ic) section. Citing no evidence that Waldheim or the Ic section in which he served had anything to do with the deportation of Jews, the report nevertheless concluded as follows:

> Lt. Waldheim's own responsibility, within the meaning of Section 212(a) (33) of the INA [the Holtzman Amendment], is clearly established. As the special missions staff officer in charge of enemy intelligence, Waldheim would have had full knowledge of the deportation operation and, very possibly, direct involvement in its planning and/or execution. His general involvement in Ic/AO operations would at the least have assisted in the persecution of Corfu Jews.[29]

Waldheim's responsibility was obviously not "clearly" established, but as will be seen, it was vital for OSI to make this claim. OSI wrongly described Waldheim's function as "special missions staff officer in charge of enemy intelligence," which in any event would not have covered matters such as deportation of Jews. The use of the expressions such as "very possibly" and "general involvement" exposed OSI's inability to implicate Waldheim in the Corfu deportations.

OSI also failed to link Waldheim to the deportation of Jews from Rhodes, referring only to a report of the intelligence branch of Commandant East Aegean, which, under the heading "counterintelligence," mentioned the deportation of Jews on instructions of Army Group E, Ic/AO and implemented by the SD. The AO section would have given such instructions, not Waldheim's office. The Commission of Historians did not even mention a possible connection between Waldheim and the deportation of the Corfu and Rhodes Jews; conversely, OSI did not refer to the Ioannina Jewish Committee report on which Wallach had relied.

(6) Army Group E – Arsakli. Charge: Waldheim's participation in the dissemination of propaganda leaflets containing anti-Semitic statements.

Basis for the charge: the initial "W" (it has not been established that it was Waldheim's) indicating receipt of a letter of transmittal relating to a package of propaganda leaflets. OSI admitted that a propaganda unit under the supervision of the counterintelligence section prepared the leaflets and sent them to Army Group E for information only. There was no proof that Waldheim had anything to do with the leaflets, and OSI could only conclude, lamely, that "Waldheim had some involvement with [the leaflets]."[30]

(7) Army Group E – Arsakli. Charge: Waldheim's participation in procedures leading to the execution of Allied commandos.

Basis for the charge: none apparent in the report. It asserted that on at least two occasions, Lt. Waldheim "personally participated in the disposition of captured Allied Commandos,"[31] but the only evidence it cited were the same documents the British Ministry of Defence had concluded did not implicate Waldheim. OSI could only claim vaguely that the documents "leave little doubt" of Waldheim's involvement.[32] Finally, in a deliberate distortion of a Waldheim brief submitted to OSI, the report found it, "to say the least, disturbing" that Waldheim, described as a "self-proclaimed champion of human rights," would seek to justify Hitler's commando order. In fact, Waldheim did not attempt to justify the order. He conceded that the order could lead to war crimes, but argued that the order had military, rather than persecutory, motivations and therefore was outside the scope of the Holtzman Amendment.[33]

(8) Anti-Guerrilla Warfare – Greece. Charge: None.

This is perhaps the strangest part of the OSI report, for it cited no specific case for Waldheim's participation in German Army reprisals against Greek guerrillas. Indeed, the report admitted that reprisals against civilians were carried out at the combat unit level with the participation of the SD and the Abwehr, but alleged, without any support, that this "raises the possibility" of Waldheim's involvement.[34]

(2) Yugoslavia – Fall 1944. Charge: Waldheim's direct responsibility for reprisal killings.

Basis for the charge: the Yugoslav War Crimes Commission Resolution (*Odluka*). When the Yugoslav file on Waldheim was opened for inspection in late 1986, OSI sent an investigator to Belgrade to examine it. OSI must have then realized that the accusations against Waldheim were politically motivated fabrications, as did the Austrian historians and Professor Herzstein. Moreover, a number of stories to this effect appeared in the press at the end of 1986, well before the report was completed. Nevertheless, OSI devoted twenty pages to the discredited Yugoslav war-crime file and accepted it at face value without any qualifications or reservations. The temptation to make use of the only document that specifically accused Waldheim of criminal acts was evidently too strong to resist. Mark Richard, the Justice Department lawyer who was the leader of the American delegation sent to Vienna in May 1987 to explain the Watch List decision, mentioned the Yugoslav file in defensive and circumspect terms at the meeting with the Austrians. He said that the file could not be dismissed out of hand; it contained information that confirmed certain aspects of the assignments and duties of Lieutenant Waldheim, even if one did not believe the war-crime accusations.[35]

Following the review of the charges against Waldheim, the report added derogatory comments on other matters irrelevant to the Watch List issue, including speculation in the press that Soviet Bloc intelligence agencies may have recruited Waldheim. Although admitting it had not investigated the matter, which in any event was not within its jurisdiction, OSI declared that such allegations should be taken seriously because all of the ingredients were present for Waldheim to have been compromised by the Soviets.[36]

The OSI report then discussed Waldheim's credibility. This was an important issue, the report asserted, because "much of what Mr. Waldheim says about his duties in the Balkans, and those of the units in which he served, is at odds with the documentation." Why Waldheim's credibility was an important issue in this context is not clear, but OSI found it useful to depict Waldheim as a liar and obfuscator. While admitting that Waldheim's failure to highlight his service in the Balkans in his books was not relevant to its inquiry under the Holtzman Amendment, OSI nevertheless devoted several pages to the subject.[37]

The report cited two other "examples" of Waldheim's lack of credibility, the first being the use of the term "ordinance" officer in several memoranda submitted by Waldheim's lawyers to OSI. According to OSI, this usage was meant to give the false impression that Waldheim was a harmless ordinance, or munitions, officer, an allegation that assumed inconceivable naiveté on the part of his advisors. Secondly, OSI found that Waldheim's assertion that he was classified as physically unfit for combat duty in 1942 was contradicted by a document he provided that showed he was declared fit for service on March 6, 1942. The difference between fitness for combat duty and fitness for service, however, seems obvious.[38]

In the final section of the report, OSI defended the pertinence of the Holtzman Amendment to Waldheim's case, which Waldheim's lawyers had challenged. That statute excludes from the United States any person who, in association with the Nazi government of Germany, "ordered, incited, assisted, or otherwise participated in the persecution of any person because of race, religion, national origin, or political opinion." That the Holtzman Amendment did not apply to any of the accusations against Waldheim except for those relating to Jews should have been obvious even to laymen. Consider the alleged mistreatment and murder of British prisoners. By no stretch of the imagination can it be argued that this mistreatment represented "persecution" because of "race, religion, national origin, or political opinion." The motivation was military, nothing more, and OSI could not explain how the Holtzman Amendment applied. The reprisals against and deportations of Yugoslav and Greek civilians were part of the German Army's war against guerrillas, and occurred not because the victims were Greeks, Yugoslavs, or Communists, but because they were considered linked to hostile acts against the German Army. OSI tried to ascribe political motivations to German reprisals because Wehrmacht documents refer to "Communist bands," but the reprisals had nothing to do with the political beliefs of the guerillas. Grasping at any straw, OSI also attempted to show that the reprisals were persecutions based on national origin because one German document precluded reprisals in an area inhabited by ethnic Germans. Ethnic Germans, however, were not shooting at German soldiers.[39]

OSI did not claim that Waldheim had "ordered" or "incited" persecutions, except in reference to the Yugoslav war-crimes file. Although the evidence was weak or nonexistent, OSI had to demonstrate that Waldheim had "assisted" or "participated" in such persecutions. To make a case, OSI had to refer repeatedly to Waldheim's presence in areas where criminal acts took place, as well as his possible knowledge of such acts, and then resort to assumptions of his involvement in acts of persecution. By doing so, OSI stretched the meaning of "assistance" and "participation" beyond any reasonable limit and exposed as cynical nonsense the U.S. government's repeated assertions to the Austrians that by law the Justice Department had no choice but to place Waldheim on the Watch List. On the contrary, it would have been fully justified in *not* doing so.

Why did OSI exceed its statutory authority? The answer seems clear. If under the Holtzman Amendment, OSI had properly restricted its investigation to the deportation of Jews and the dissemination of anti-Semitic propaganda, the weakness of its case for placing the Austrian chief of state on the Watch List would have been apparent. Unwilling to rely solely on the charges relating to Jews, OSI decided to cover all the WJC accusations, even if they did not involve persecutions under the Holtzman Amendment. The report would thus paint such a villainous portrait of Waldheim that it would be impossible not to believe in his guilt, as Ambassador Lauder declared in 1987.[40] Therefore no one would be likely to quibble about OSI stretching the law. The inclusion of the portfolio of gruesome photographs, with no attempt to link them to Waldheim, as well as the reference to Waldheim's possible role as a Soviet agent, were obviously part of this effort.

For the Justice Department, the forced release of OSI's tendentious report could have been a major source of embarrassment, if the media had subjected it to a minimum of critical analysis. However, the press coverage was limited to reporting the OSI side of the Waldheim story. OSI saw to it that its version would be the first to reach the press through carefully timed and selected releases. On March 11, the day the report was disclosed, Reuters' James Vicini had already described excerpts from the OSI document presenting Waldheim in the worst possible light.

In *The Washington Post's* lead article on the release of the report,[41] staff writer Thomas Lippman's summary sounded as though it might have emanated from Eli Rosenbaum: "The portrait of Waldheim that emerges from the report is that of a canny and amoral functionary who went out of his way to sacrifice innocent victims on the altar of his ambition." The comment was not only overblown, but grossly unfair. If Waldheim had any ambition during his service in the Balkans, it was to survive the war and spend as much time as possible in

Vienna to finish his law studies and to be with his new bride. On the other hand, Lippman correctly observed that OSI made no effort to be evenhanded, describing the report as "a relentless condemnation of Waldheim and an attack on his credibility, similar to what a prosecutor would present at a trial." He did not point out that there was no trial, and Waldheim had no opportunity to challenge the OSI conclusions.

The *New York Times*[42] and Reuters[43] articles summarized the OSI document without comment, reporting in addition that the WJC had been one of the parties seeking to compel the release of the Report under the Freedom of Information Act. This false information, no doubt passed to the press by the WJC and OSI, served to portray the WJC as an adversary of OSI, rather than the close ally that it, in fact, was. The cozy relationship between the two organizations was a source of potential embarrassment for the Justice Department, but the press did not report on the role Rosenbaum's book had played in the decision to release the OSI report.

In another piece of disinformation, a Justice Department spokesman told *The Washington Post* that the report was released because Attorney General Janet Reno had "relaxed the department's secrecy guidelines."[44] The report's chief author, Neal Sher, had left OSI a month earlier to become director of the American-Israeli Political Action Committee (AIPAC), one of the most formidable pressure groups in Washington.[45] The Justice Department denied that this move had anything to do with the release of the report.[46] Rosenbaum succeeded Sher as director of OSI.

Mapother was disappointed that the OSI report had been portrayed to the American public as a serious and convincing indictment of Waldheim. To him, it was obviously a dishonest piece of prosecutorial nonsense, particularly in its reliance on the discredited Yugoslav war crimes file. Mapother decided to try to redress the balance. He managed to persuade David Binder, a senior *New York Times* Washington correspondent and an old friend of his, to write an article exposing the report's flaws. Mapother put Binder in touch with Professor Herzstein, who had also criticized the report. Binder prepared a draft article based on Herzstein's and Mapother's analyses and received a preliminary go-ahead from his superiors in New York, subject to his reviewing the draft with Neal Sher.

Sher refused to comment on specific criticisms of the report and tried to discourage Binder from going ahead with the article. While completing the draft, Binder received telephone calls from Elan Steinberg of the WJC and from Sher, urging him to drop the story. He nevertheless sent his final draft to New York, but it never found its way to print. The story was killed at the *Times* headquarters because, Binder was told, it had ceased to be newsworthy.[47]

Waldheim was no longer president of Austria when the OSI report was released, his term having expired in 1992. Nevertheless, the Austrians continued to seek the reversal of the Watch List decision, which they always viewed as unjust. On April 26, 1994, the Austrian Embassy issued a press release announcing it had requested the Department of Justice to rescind the Watch List decision in view of the unfounded allegations of the OSI report.[48] Attached to the Embassy's request was a six-page memorandum pointing out the errors and distortions in the report. The Justice Department did not respond to the Austrian arguments and tersely notified the Embassy that the Watch List decision would stand.[49] Despite the press release, the Austrian demarche to the U.S. government on behalf of Waldheim received no coverage at all in the mainstream American press.[50]

Three months after the release of the OSI report, Pope John Paul II conferred a papal knighthood on the ex-president of Austria for his services to peace during his tenure as UN Secretary General. The cries of outrage from Jewish organizations and from the government of Israel were as loud—and as overwrought—as those generated by the pope's decision to meet with Waldheim in 1987.[51] A group of congressmen addressed a letter to the Vatican representative in Washington demanding that the papal award be rescinded. They inaccurately claimed that historical analysis had revealed that Waldheim had directly engaged in acts of Nazi brutality.[52] Despite the release of the OSI report, Waldheim's image in the U.S. remained unchanged. The public was left—and remains—uninformed.

Although the release of the OSI report confirmed the lack of any substance behind the accusations regarding his Balkan military service, the story of the Waldheim affair would not be complete without an examination of the subsidiary accusations against him: that he was a Nazi and a liar.

CHAPTER VIII

"A Nazi and a Liar"

On March 25, 1986, as the anti-Waldheim campaign gained momentum, newspaper reporters filled the small conference room at WJC headquarters in New York City to capacity. With much fanfare, Singer, Steinberg, and Rosenbaum introduced Professor Herzstein to the assembled representatives of the press. It was announced that the professor had made some dramatic discoveries at the National Archives. These discoveries allegedly linked Waldheim to the liquidation of allied prisoners of war and to the massacres of Yugoslav partisans. The documents that Herzstein presented, however, did not involve Waldheim personally in war crimes. Singer, perhaps sensing the reporters were not convinced, declared at the end of the conference: "Our first accusation is that Kurt Waldheim was a Nazi... We have proven that point beyond a shadow of a doubt. We have proven as well that Kurt Waldheim is a liar. We have proven that beyond a shadow of a doubt."[1] These were strong words, and the accusations have continued to haunt Waldheim even as the war-crime charges fell by the wayside.

Was Waldheim really the "Nazi" and "liar" the WJC claimed, or were these constantly repeated accusations used as a smokescreen to hide the weakness of the war-crime charges? The allegation that Waldheim was a Nazi stemmed from two principal sources: notations in his military service record and an unsigned judicial service personnel form indicating membership in the National Socialist Riding Corps (*SA Reiterstandarte*) and in the National Socialist Student Union while he was a student at the Consular Academy.[2]

Waldheim has denied that he voluntarily joined either organization, and neither of the membership lists included his name. The reference to the Riding Corps resulted from the automatic incorporation of most equestrian organizations, including Waldheim's, into the SA (*Sturmabteilung*). This inclusion followed the *Anschluss* and occurred without the consent of the members.

When Waldheim applied for a position in the Austrian civil service after the end of the war, he mentioned the Riding Corps affiliation on his questionnaire, which required disclosure of Nazi organization memberships. The Austrian authorities subsequently informed Waldheim that his record was clear and that he was not subject to anti-Nazi sanctions. These sanctions were applicable only to individuals who had voluntarily joined the SA.[3]

As for the National Socialist Student Union, it has never been considered a proscribed Nazi organization giving rise to sanctions against its members.[4] Even assuming that Waldheim had voluntarily joined the Student Union, membership alone would not have been an indication of his adherence to Nazi ideology. In 1979, the Berlin Document Center, a U.S. controlled central repository of Nazi-organization membership documents, reported to Simon Wiesenthal that no record of Kurt Waldheim existed in its files.[5]

Positive evidence exists that Waldheim and his family, far from being Nazis or Nazi sympathizers, were in fact hostile to the National Socialists. Waldheim's father was persecuted for his anti-Nazi views as a school teacher and was forced out of his job.[6] In 1940, the Nazi provincial (*Gau*) office responsible for the Waldheim family residence issued a declaration to the judicial authorities in Vienna certifying that Kurt Waldheim, along with his parents, had openly expressed hostility toward the Nazi movement.[7]

Lord Weidenfeld, a prominent English Jew who emigrated from Austria prior to World War II, has chronicled Waldheim's attitude toward the Nazis and anti-Semitism. In his autobiography, *Remembering My Good Friends*,[8] Weidenfeld describes his acquaintance with Waldheim while studying at the Vienna Consular Academy at the time of the Anschluss: "[Kurt Waldheim's] father was a functionary of the Catholic Patriotic Front, a cog in the wheel of the *Schuschnigg* establishment, a devout Christian and anti-Nazi. Kurt wanted to become a lawyer and a diplomat. He kept to himself, attended all seminars and made himself agreeable to all and sundry. We sometimes met with a charming Dutch fellow student, Suzanne K., a staunch patriot and hater of the Nazis. Waldheim was known as a pillar of the Catholic regime... It was only after the Anschluss that I got to know him better. He was one of the very few who did not change his attitude to the students of Jewish descent. In fact, he rendered me some invaluable services. During the five months between the *Anschluss* and my departure from Vienna, a complex compromise between the German Ministry of Education and the Foreign Ministry meant that Jewish students at the *Konsularakademie* were allowed to sit for examinations, but not to attend lectures. Since there were few textbooks, lecture notes were essential for the exams. This made life for the Jews more difficult. Waldheim brought lecture notes to my house, a favor which required some courage, all the more so since my father was a prisoner of the German Reich... If the motive behind the attacks on Waldheim were to rouse the world to the Austrians' inadequate sense of responsibility for and compassion for the victims of the Holocaust, then Kurt Waldheim was not the most suitable target."[9]

Weidenfeld had expressed similar views in the following sworn statement he made on Waldheim's behalf in 1986:

> During our common time of studies, Kurt Waldheim was generally known as an active liberal Catholic and convinced anti-Nazi who...voiced definitely anti-racist views and had many Jewish friends... Also, I kept up continuous contacts with Dr. Kurt Waldheim after the war and was able to convince myself that he has kept to the above explained view of things unchanged until today.[10]

The "Nazi" accusation proved to be so baseless that the WJC gradually stopped calling Waldheim a Nazi, but the damage had been done. The U.S. press continued to refer to Waldheim's "Nazi past," "Nazi ties," and "Nazi role," describing him as "this one-time servant of the Nazi onslaught," and "ex-Nazi trooper Waldheim."[11]

From the beginning of its campaign against Waldheim, the WJC charged that he had deliberately concealed and lied about his military service in the Balkans because he feared its disclosure would have adversely affected his career, and OSI used the "credibility" issue in an attempt to bolster its case. The cover-up charge was often couched in suspiciously sensational terms. Rosenbaum asserted that Waldheim had perpetrated "one of the most elaborate deceptions of our time" and termed it "the international political cover-up of the century."[12]

According to his accusers, Waldheim wanted the public to believe that his military service ended on his return to Austria after being wounded in Russia in 1941 in an effort to conceal his Balkan assignments. First, in *The Challenge of Peace*, his 1977 book describing his first term at the UN, Waldheim stated that he was medically discharged after his leg wound, resumed his law studies and obtained his doctorate two years later. This book was originally written in French by a ghost writer, Eric Rouleau of the French newspaper *Le Monde*, and appeared under the title *Un Metier Unique au Monde*. The French version referred to Waldheim's repatriation but did not claim that he was medically discharged. The use of this phrase in the English version seems to have been a translation error. Neither version mentioned service in the Balkans.[13]

Secondly, in 1980, Congressman Solarz of New York wrote to Waldheim, who was then UN Secretary General, concerning allegations that he had been involved in the Nazi Youth Movement and that he had not been forthcoming about his activities with his unit or units on the Soviet front. Solarz requested that Waldheim provide him with the names of the units with which he had served during the years 1939-1945.

In his reply to Solarz, Waldheim denied any participation in the Nazi Youth Movement and referred only to his unit on the Russian front. He concluded with the statement, "Being incapacitated from further service at the front, I resumed my law studies at Vienna University, where I graduated in 1944."

What Waldheim wrote was, in fact, true. He was declared unfit for combat duty, and he did complete his law studies in Vienna during a number of study leaves during the years 1942-44. But since he did not list the units he served with in the Balkans during those years, his reply implied that his military service ended with his Russian experience. However, Solarz's letter had focused on Waldheim's Soviet-front activities (he asked about extermination units, which were a phenomenon of that particular area) so Waldheim may have thought that the congressman was only interested in that aspect of Waldheim's military career.[14] In any event, Waldheim, irritated by the peremptory tone of Solarz's letter (it demanded Waldheim's "immediate attention"), was not inclined to be expansive in his reply.[15]

Finally, in his 1985 book, *In the Eye of the Storm*,[16] in which he described his career as Secretary General of the UN, Waldheim mentioned only his Soviet-front experience, adding that after his injury in 1941, he was discharged from further service at the front, a true, though incomplete, statement.

The German version of Waldheim's book contained the following language:

"Upon termination of my study leave and after recovering from my leg injury, I was recalled to army service. Shortly before the end of the war, I was in the area of Trieste."[17]

This passage had originally been included in the English edition as well, but the English publisher deleted it to shorten the text.[18] Waldheim had also briefly referred to his post-1942 military service in campaign brochures during his unsuccessful bid for the Austrian presidency in 1971 and mentioned his Balkan service in the course of a talk he gave at the Aldo Moro Institute in Rome on October 4, 1985.[19]

The cover-up charge raised a number of questions that its proponents did not address:

- If Waldheim were afraid that his UN career would have been jeopardized by a disclosure of his Balkan service, why did the three documents (the 1977 book; the 1980 letter to Solarz; and the 1985 book) cited as proof of the cover-up appear only during and after his second and last term as UN Secretary General?
- If Waldheim had intended to conceal his assignments in the Balkans, why did he make references, however sketchy, to his return to service after recovering from his wound?
- Was it really likely that Waldheim, an intelligent man, would have engaged in a cover-up that was doomed to failure? His personal military records, listing all his assignments, were available in various archives as the WJC research effort demonstrated, and numerous fellow servicemen had witnessed his presence in the Balkans.

Waldheim's writings undeniably emphasized his Soviet front experience, while at the same time downplaying or disregarding his subsequent Balkan service. Leaving aside the erroneous reference to his medical discharge in the English translation of his 1977 book, Waldheim gave incomplete accounts of his post-1941 war years, but he did not lie about them. He has explained that the combat experience in Russia, which nearly cost him his life, was, in his view, the most dramatic part of his military service and overshadowed the interpreting and office functions he performed later as a junior staff officer. On the eastern front, Waldheim had served in one of the rare cavalry reconnaissance units of the German Army, whose highly dangerous mission was to fan out ahead of the infantry in order to draw enemy fire and thus pinpoint the location of Soviet troops. For him, obtaining his doctorate and getting married were the important events during the years 1942-45. He did not see any reason (or obligation, for that matter) to dwell at length on his military service in books that did not purport to be complete autobiographies but that related only to his diplomatic and United Nations career. Not surprisingly, Waldheim considered his service as a junior staff lieutenant of no particular interest to the general public.

Waldheim may have foreseen that his political opponents might seize upon his presence during the "dirty" Balkan war as a basis for attacking him. Waldheim has admitted that giving the impression of sweeping his Balkan service under the rug was a serious blunder; it enabled his accusers to mask their inability to demonstrate any wrongdoing on his part by claiming that he must have wanted to hide some dark secret.

In three negative editorials during the first half of 1986, *The New York*

Times, while admitting the documents produced by the WJC did not prove Waldheim had been involved in war crimes, claimed that his Balkan service had been "mendaciously" covered up and made his explanations suspect. The concealment of that service, the *Times,* alleged, was self-indicting: Waldheim was guilty, regardless of proof.[20]

Although superficially plausible, the cover-up theory made no sense. The records of Waldheim's military service existed from the very beginning in official archives. No one has alleged that he tried to destroy them, and they were available to investigators. Moreover, on the only occasion he was officially required to do so, Waldheim disclosed his Balkan service. When he applied for entry into the Austrian Civil Service at the end of 1945, his application form indicated that his military service lasted from 1939 through May 9, 1945, and that he had served in France, Russia, and the Balkans. In an attached curriculum vitae, he declared that he had served in the Wehrmacht on the "Eastern, Western, Southern, and Southeastern fronts until the end of the war." These documents remained in his personnel file in Vienna.[21] How, then, could his failure to emphasize such service in his writings possibly be viewed as a "mendacious deception of historical proportions?"

Waldheim was also accused of lying about a number of aspects of his Balkan service. Waldheim had first maintained, in April 1986, that he had not been present during the German campaign against the Yugoslav partisans in the Kozara Mountains. He corrected his statement a few months later, explaining that he had more than ten different assignments in the Balkans, and it was not surprising that after more than forty years, he could be mistaken in his dates.

Rosenbaum believed that Waldheim was deliberately trying to conceal his participation in the Kozara campaign,[22] but this assertion assumes incredible stupidity on Waldheim's part. He knew his military service in the Balkans was being examined in minute detail.

Simon Wiesenthal defended Waldheim during the WJC campaign, but he broke ranks with him on one issue, Waldheim's denial of any contemporaneous knowledge of the deportation of the Salonika Jews. "I cannot believe you," he told Waldheim in 1986, but stopped short of calling him a liar.[23] Waldheim's absence from Salonika at the time of the deportations would seem like a reasonable explanation for his claimed lack of knowledge, but curiously, his absence did not satisfy Wiesenthal, as it had not satisfied historian Yehuda Wallach. The issue was, in any event, irrelevant to the question of Waldheim's guilt, as it was clear that Waldheim could not have been involved in the Salonika deportations. For Wiesenthal, though, it affected Waldheim's credibility to such an extent that Wiesenthal called for Waldheim's resignation following the release of the historians' report. No one has explained, however, why Waldheim would have risked a lie, when admitting the truth would have done him no harm.

CHAPTER IX

Closing Remarks

Kurt Waldheim's term as president of Austria ended in July 1992. Thomas Klestil, the People's Party candidate in the 1992 elections, succeeded him. As Austrian ambassador in Washington, Klestil had tried unsuccessfully to keep Waldheim off the Watch List. During the electoral campaign, both Klestil and his Socialist opponent defended Waldheim. Klestil promised to continue the effort to rescind the Watch List decision. The Justice Department, however, refused to reopen the Waldheim case following the release of the OSI report. The U.S. Embassy in Vienna rebuffed any attempt to revive the issue and arrogantly declared that the Austrians would be better off forgetting about it.[1]

The Austrians have not forgotten, least of all Kurt Waldheim. After his retirement, he wrote a book entitled *Die Antwort (The Answer)*,[2] which was published in Vienna in June 1996. Giving his side of the story, Waldheim expressed bitterness over his treatment by the American government as well as astonishment at the virulence of the WJC onslaught and its amplification by the American media. The book received little publicity in the United States. *The New York Post*, in an editorial, alleged that Waldheim had "processed orders for the mass deportation of Greek Jews to Auschwitz," and castigated Waldheim for blaming his predicament on a Jewish conspiracy.[3]

Conspiracy or not, the WJC, supported by most of the world Jewish community and Israel, undoubtedly spearheaded the campaign to prevent Waldheim's election as president and, when that failed, to place him on the Watch List. Although the WJC claimed it was pursuing Waldheim to expose him as a Nazi war criminal who had persecuted Jews it apparently had other motives as well.

Early in his book, *Betrayal*, Rosenbaum wrote that as UN Secretary General, "Waldheim had provided observers with considerable evidence that he was hostile to Israel in particular and to Jewish interests in general."[4] He cited Waldheim's refusal to cover his head during a Holocaust remembrance ceremony in Israel. He also referred to Yasir Arafat's appearance before the UN General Assembly and the passage of a resolution by that body equating Zionism with racism even though, as Secretary General, Waldheim was powerless to thwart the will of the General Assembly. Rosenbaum also criticized Waldheim's statement to the press that the Israeli raid on Entebbe to free hostages was a violation of Ugandan territorial sovereignty, but failed to note that Waldheim had added that in this case the violation was justified for humanitarian reasons.[5]

Curiously, Rosenbaum did not refer to Waldheim's sympathy for the aspirations of the Palestinian people or his criticism of Israel's invasion of Lebanon. Waldheim was reflecting the Austrian tradition of supporting Palestinian rights, which Socialist Chancellor Bruno Kreisky, who was himself of Jewish origin, had also championed. In *Die Antwort*,[6] Waldheim denied that he personally favored the Arab over the Israeli side in the various Middle East conflicts with which he had to deal. When he opposed Israeli actions in Lebanon, he was again reflecting the consensus of the UN. For Israel's most vocal supporters in the United States, any criticism of Israel was considered unforgivable, if not anti-Semitic. Accusations of Waldheim as war criminal thus fell on fertile ground.

Edgar Bronfman, as head of the WJC, has sought to preserve its reputation as one of the highest profile Jewish organizations. The WJC, therefore, needed to sponsor well-publicized "causes" such as the Waldheim affair and later, the attack on the Swiss banks. While boasting that the campaign against "that despicable liar Kurt Waldheim" was "terrific publicity" for the WJC, Bronfman asserted that the principal motivation in attacking Waldheim as a Nazi war criminal was to redirect world attention to the Holocaust, to ensure that it would not be forgotten, and to counter Holocaust revisionism. That Waldheim had nothing to do with the Holocaust did not seem to bother Bronfman as long as the press reported the WJC accusations of Waldheim's alleged role in sending Greek Jews to Auschwitz. Like the OSI, he never acknowledged the phony nature of the Yugoslav war-crime charges. On the contrary, he cited the same charges in 1996 as an example of Waldheim's atrocious wartime behavior.[8]

Engaging in a witch-hunt to preserve the memory of the Holocaust can only be counterproductive. If anything, it adds grist to the mill of the revisionists. Why, people may well ask, is it necessary to defend the Holocaust with lies?[9] Indeed, a remarkable aspect of the Waldheim affair is how it became such a burning issue for Jewish organizations in the United States despite its total lack of a credible Holocaust connection.

Other Jewish groups, as well as the State of Israel, generally supported the attack of the WJC on Waldheim. When the Vatican received President Waldheim in 1987, the American Jewish Congress, the Synagogue Council of America, the

B'nai B'rith Anti-Defamation League and the American Jewish Committee joined the WJC in excoriating the pope.[10] Voices critical of the WJC were rarely heard, the most prominent being that of Simon Wiesenthal. Defending Waldheim, he openly criticized the WJC for its amateurish methods of Nazi hunting. Indeed, he expressed amazement at how, without any rationale save for the zeal of the WJC and its media supporters, the Waldheim matter became the biggest Nazi war-criminal story since the Eichmann trial. [11] As a result, he incurred the wrath of the WJC, which Rosenbaum relates in his book and accounts for its title, *Betrayal.* According to Wiesenthal, a WJC vice president declared at a conference in Geneva in April of 1986, "Waldheim, who sent Jews to the gas chambers, is being supported and defended by the prominent Jew, Simon Wiesenthal."[12]

In 1992, Wiesenthal, Lord Weidenfeld, and Michael Wolffsohn, a history professor, published an article in *The Jerusalem Post* entitled "Just Who Are Our Jewish Leaders?" The article criticized Bronfman and the WJC for their irresponsibility and their irrelevance:

> Though the Waldheim case may have been the WJC's most important problem for the past six years (despite its inability to substantiate its charges with concrete evidence) these actions, in fact, only distract from the real problems of our time, such as hatred of Jews, neo-Nazism, anti-Semitism in some post-communist countries, the essential issue of a peace settlement between Israel and its Arab neighbors, and so on.[13]

Wiesenthal was never forgiven for breaking ranks in the Waldheim affair. In a 1996 German television program on Wiesenthal, Rosenbaum said that the closest the Nazi hunter ever came to a Nazi war criminal was Kurt Waldheim.

In the eyes of the WJC, Professor Herzstein also became a traitor to the cause. After his stint as a researcher for the WJC, he wrote a book on Waldheim's early years. The book exposed the trumped-up Yugoslav charges and presented, with one exception, a balanced account of Waldheim's Balkan service. Although Hertzstein's account did not implicate Waldheim personally with any wrongdoing, it made a strained attempt to link him to the persecution of Jews.[14] For this, Herzstein had to rely (as did Wallach in the historians report) on the only document bearing Waldheim's signature that mentioned Jews: a copy of a long radio message from a German field unit to the German liaison staff in Athens, where Waldheim was serving. Among numerous other items, it dealt with partisan activities and mentioned that "Ioannina and the Jewish community there could be seen as a center for preparing an uprising." Waldheim had initialed a copy for the staff's files, to certify its authenticity.

There was no evidence that the Germans took any action against the "Jewish community" as a result of the radio message. Yet on the basis of the document alone, Herzstein melodramatically concluded that Waldheim "had played a small but necessary role in the smooth execution of Hitler's Final Solution" and had "served as an efficient and effective cog in the machinery of genocide."[15] Herzstein admitted later in his book that Waldheim's personal involvement with the Holocaust was "minimal."[16] How could the playing of a "necessary role" be "minimal" involvement?

Despite its contribution to Holocaust remembrance, Rosenbaum considered Herzstein's book as far too favorable toward Waldheim and dismissed it with the comment that the book could best be appraised by the endorsement on its cover: "Absolutely brilliant—Simon Wiesenthal."[17] Subsequently Herzstein told David Binder of *The New York Times* that the OSI report was flawed and came close to getting Waldheim for political reasons[18]—more treachery, of course.

One Israeli has publicly expressed his concern for the harmful effects the WJC actions against Waldheim had on Austria's Jewish community and on Israel's foreign policy. Shlomo Avineri, a professor of political science at the Hebrew University of Jerusalem and a former director general of the Israeli Ministry of Foreign Affairs, in an article entitled "The Waldheim Affair—How the World Jewish Congress Blew It," deplored the unprofessional way in which the WJC had attacked Waldheim. Avineri argued that the WJC, because of its high profile, should not have involved the Jewish community in general and the State of Israel in an unnecessary diplomatic confrontation with Austria.[19] He could have said the same about the WJC's pressure on the U.S. government, which also led to a pointless conflict with Austria.

Without the support of the American media, especially *The New York Times* and *The Washington Post*, the WJC would not have been able to promote the false "Nazi war criminal" image of Waldheim in the United States. The American press did not distinguish itself in the Waldheim affair. In contrast the leading German-language newspapers in Europe, such as the *Frankfurter Allgemeine Zeitung* and the *Neue Zuercher Zeitung*, were generally skeptical of the WJC accusations. The American reporting, as has been shown, was often biased, inaccurate, or incomplete. True, the Waldheim story was unusually complex and required much research for a proper understanding, but this complexity cannot excuse the one-sided opinions that emanated from editorial desks.

The New York Times, beginning with John Tagliabue's March 4, 1986 article, provided the launching pad for the WJC campaign. The newspaper thereafter buttressed its news coverage with anti-Waldheim editorials. In March 1986, the *Times* declared:

> Daily come fresh charges—and denials—concerning the wartime activities of Kurt Waldheim, the former Secretary General of the United Nations. Mr. Waldheim, who is running for president of Austria, says the evidence of his service to the Nazis is stale stuff, the fruit of a conspiracy and, in any case, overblown. His nonchalance is staggering, and his denials are disingenuous.[20]

If Waldheim had done no wrong, his nonchalance would not have been staggering, nor would his denials have been disingenuous. The *Times* had already decided Waldheim had indeed been guilty of something in the Balkans, if not specifically of war crimes. The paper was not prepared to give him any benefit of a doubt. After the election, the *Times* blamed the Austrians for placing "a conspicuously flawed figure on their highest pedestal."[21]

A year later, Jewish groups in the United States verbally attacked the Pope for having received President Waldheim at the Vatican. The *Times* pitched in with a critical editorial entitled, "Austria's Albatross, at the Vatican." The editorial did admit, however, that the event had given rise to "overwrought oratory." Engaging in more than a little of the same, the editorial declared that the Pope's failure to express disapproval of Waldheim's wartime service had the effect of "slighting all the victims of Hitler's war" and that the reputations of Austria and the Vatican were "tarnished by this former lieutenant who had forgotten much and learned little." The *Times* editorial mistakenly noted that Waldheim had been put on the Watch List "because he concealed his war record."[22]

The *Times* also failed to do its homework. Following the issuance of the report of the International Commission of Historians, the paper accused Waldheim of engaging in a "niggardly parsing of guilt and innocence" because he claimed that the report exonerated him. Instead of facing the truth, the editorial added, Waldheim "squirms and runs. His cowardice is Austria's loss."[23] It appears that no one at the *Times* had read the full text of the historians' report or understood it if they did.

On March 31, 1992, *The New York Times* aimed one more jab at President Waldheim, whose term was about to expire. Prime Minister Streibl of Bavaria had invited him to lunch with German Chancellor Helmut Kohl, thus provoking angry protests from Jewish leaders. The *Times* supported the Jewish leaders with an editorial that referred to a "chief of state notorious for lying about his service in the Nazi war machine" and to "an Austrian who still cannot remember just what he did as an intelligence officer in the brutal Balkan campaign." The *Times* continued to avoid specifically accusing Waldheim of war crimes, but its insinuations were obviously intended to lead readers to that conclusion. In passing, the newspaper took a swipe at Chancellor Kohl, a long-time defender of Waldheim, and described him as "provocatively callous" for having declared that he needed no advice on whom to meet.[24]

In addition to the editorials, *New York Times* columnist A. M. Rosenthal regularly attacked Waldheim in his columns.[25] As late as 1996, Rosenthal referred to Waldheim as a "war-crimes suspect" on the basis of the long discredited Yugoslav file.[26] Other *Times* writers—William Safire, Anthony Lewis, and Flora Lewis, also produced anti-Waldheim pieces. The *Times* opened its op-ed pages almost exclusively to Waldheim critics, including Professor Amos Perlmutter of American University, Bronfman, Rabbis Hier and Cooper, and Arthur J. Goldberg.[27] Bronfman used the *Times* in 1988 to charge that Waldheim, clearly immoral and without a conscience, was a "liar and an unrepentant man who was part and parcel of the Nazi killing machine."[28]

At *The Washington Post*, the attitude was much the same. Although the Post finally agreed in 1992 to print a short article by John Mapother questioning the conventional wisdom on Waldheim in the United States,[29] its editorials and commentary ran uniformly against the Austrian president.[30] Richard Cohen, a *Post* columnist, reached new heights of anti-Waldheim nonsense in a column decrying the Pope's award to him in 1994.[31] He described Waldheim as a "liar whose complicity in the Holocaust, no matter how passive, he never acknowledged." He did not explain what he meant by passive complicity—to be an accomplice would seem to exclude passivity—let alone the concept of degrees of passivity. He became even more incomprehensible when he added that "(Waldheim) was a careerist who punched a ticket through the Holocaust."

The *Post* has not relented in its attacks on Waldheim. In December 1997, Representative Tom Lantos of California, from the beginning one of Waldheim's fiercest critics, likened Donald Smalz to Kurt Waldheim. Smalz, the special counsel investigating former Agriculture Secretary Mike Espy, also had an alleged lapse of memory, hence the comparison. Lantos's silly remark provoked a long editorial in the *Post* expressing outrage at the "unfair verbal assault" on Smalz, who "certainly deserve(d) better than comparison to Kurt Waldheim."[32]

Why did the most respected newspapers in the United States handle the Waldheim story so one-sidedly? One possible explanation is that the press in general tends to print what is likely to appeal most to the public. Nazi war criminal stories always make good copy, and the more villainous a villain, the better. Moreover, *The New York Times* must have found it difficult to remain objective after joining forces with the WJC in February 1986 to expose Waldheim. Its editorials suggest that the newspaper adopted the WJC position early in the game and stuck to it for the duration. Would Waldheim have ended up on the Watch List if the leading American newspapers had been more even-handed in their handling of the Waldheim affair? One can only speculate, but it seems reasonable to assume that the relentless press barrage created a political environment conducive to the sanctioning of the Austrian president by the U.S. government.

Waldheim has continued to be a source of political capital for members of Congress. Representative Carolyn B. Maloney, a New York Democrat, sponsored legislation in 1994, which became law in 1998, obliging the CIA to open up its files to investigators of Nazi war criminals "like Kurt Waldheim," who, she said, was directly involved in the deportation and murder of the Jews.[33] Maloney was inspired by A. M. Rosenthal who had alleged that the CIA file on Waldheim contained damning information on his past. He also argued that the U.S. government should not be allowed to protect him.[34] In view of the intensive investigations to which the Waldheim affair has been subjected, it is highly unlikely that the CIA file would contain anything new. Also unlikely, however, is that the disclosure of a "clean" CIA file on Waldheim would change his image in the United States. John Mapother, a CIA veteran, was told by friends in the U.S. government that the State Department, the Defense Department, and the CIA suppressed distribution of any Waldheim material that failed to corroborate the WJC charges. If true, this constituted a disservice to justice which requires that the truth be revealed.

And what of the OSI? The continued existence within the Department of Justice of an organization so intimately tied to a particular constituency raises the prospect of other misapplications of the law; why should the U.S. taxpayers continue to support an organization responsible for the Demjanjuk scandal and whose most recent directors, Sher and Rosenbaum, cited as one of its greatest achievements the placing of the Austrian President on the Watch List? There must surely be a better way of dealing with Nazi war criminals in the United States, if any still exist.

Since leaving the Hofburg Place in 1992, Kurt Waldheim has been quietly living in Vienna with his wife, Sissy. Their apartment, in a building which at one time served as guest quarters for the Austro-Hungarian Emperor, is tastefully furnished with antiques collected over the years by the Waldheims. In summer, they move to their lakeside villa on the Attersee near Salzburg, where they enjoy the visits of their children and grandchildren.

The Waldheim family ties, always close, were further strengthened as a consequence of the witch hunt. Waldheim's son Gerhard interrupted his banking career in 1986 and 1987 to spend many months defending his father in the United States and in Austria. Waldheim's wife and two daughters, Liselotte and Christa, provided him with much-needed affection and moral support during the darkest period of those years, as did his three school-age grandsons, bewildered at first by the uproar concerning their grandfather's past. Waldheim paid homage to his family's loyalty and trust in a moving dedication for his 1996 book, *"Die Antwort"*.

As befits an elder statesman (he is now 82 years old), Waldheim remains actively interested in Austrian political, cultural and social life, and his tall, silver-haired figure continues to be a familiar sight in Viennese circles. Through the Austrian League for the United Nations, which he heads, he has pursued his primary interest in foreign affairs and occasionally lectures on UN and European Union matters.

Waldheim should be thoroughly enjoying his retirement years, but the picture is not complete. The galling effects of the witch hunt still continue to haunt him: he is still barred from entering the United States and avoids visiting European countries where his enemies are likely to provoke unpleasant incidents. As clearly comes through in *"Die Antwort"*, he is a deeply hurt man who will never be happy until the tenacious ghost of the Watch List is exorcised and the damage to his reputation is undone.

Dr. Waldheim has been out of the international limelight for many years, and his name probably only evokes dim memories in the minds of most Americans. Relations between the Unites States and Austria have returned to normal, although the Watch List decision still rankles in Vienna. So why should Americans care about what happened to Waldheim thirteen years ago? The answer, I think, is clear: the U.S. government treated him unjustly, and since it acted on behalf of the American people, they will remain parties to this injustice until it is redressed.

DEMOCRACY SUBVERTED

The Publisher's Comment

The sensational accusations against Kurt Waldheim rampaged through the American media and were propelled throughout the world with a seemingly irreversible momentum. That the former Secretary General of the United Nations was charged with being a Nazi and with atrocities and war crimes when he was a Wehrmacht officer, was big news. It was exploited for the attention it gained by the media and by the accusers. Deep feelings were aroused concerning the monstrous evils of the Nazi government in Germany and its principle crime, The Holocaust. Anti-Semitism has been an unholy act of Christian civilizations. The Nazis rallied it to their vile perversions. The charges against the distinguished Dr. Waldheim created shock and outrage. The outrage fueled the momentum in the media and then popular belief. This is all understandable.

Peter Drucker wrote that amateur business executives glory in their accomplishments while professionals analyze their mistakes. Professionals also admit their mistakes for that brings the most wholesome outcome for individuals, communities and nations. Honesty dissolves cynicism and preserves credibility.

It is certain, that the American media made mistakes. They failed to check the story in historical and military terms, and adopted the data provided by Waldheim's accusers. If *The New York Times* evaluated the first news report with their usual scrutiny, red flags would have been planted all over it. It was, however, a really big story. John Tagliabue and his editors put too much trust in the word of Eli Rosenbaum. Other icons of American television and print did the same. The American people were never fully informed.

As for Rosenbaum and Neil Sher, they allowed speculation to become what they considered to be reality. This is a heady phenomena. The intriguing and persuasive discussion that results, leads usually to erroneous conclusions. Napoleon warned that the most grievous mistake a general could make is to project a battlefield situation and then assume it is intelligence. Rosenbaum and Sher needed to be sure at least of their sources. They had incomplete information and failed to recognize it. With unproven speculation they allowed themselves to accuse Kurt Waldheim of guilt-by-association in the most egregious form.

Time was needed to organize a proper response. Ask anyone over 65 where they were more than 40 years ago. It is not easy to reconstruct events. Documents are difficult to find. Recollections have to be checked. Because of his strong anti-Nazi record and feelings Waldheim couldn't believe what was happening at first. During the delay, the speculative story that had been passed off as news assumed veracity.

Dr. Waldheim never had the opportunity to review, much less respond to the "evidence" the OSI used to recommend that he be placed on the INS Watch List. When facts are ignored, manipulated, distorted and concealed by the Justice Department of the United States, American democracy is seriously jeopardized. The Justice Department is supposed to set the standard for investigatory impartiality. The OSI pandered to another agenda.

The White House also made mistakes. The Reagan Administration and Attorney General Edwin Meese failed to control and press the investigation to determine the truth. Government in democracy has the ultimate responsibility for the truth. Any of the key figures or President Reagan himself could have stopped the process and focused attention on the facts and the truth. They did not. They chose not to risk the ire of the Jewish community or the vocal part of it in this matter.

But it is for all of us to risk whatever we must to assure that false perceptions do not dominate society. The American talent for advertising and public relations makes us a country where perceptions of all types are created. These talents have long been used in politics. They should never be abused.

The causes and effects of the boom in tabloid television and tabloid news are complex, but as many journalists and publishers have affirmed, the standards have suffered. It is now more important to compete for the audience than to be sure of the truth of what was being reported. If it was in *The New York Times*, it must be credible.

The action against Kurt Waldheim unintentionally became a "big lie." This manifested in repetition as "big lies" do. Intentional false perceptions are things of fascism and totalitarianism. They are a means of control and manipulation. Intentional or unintentional big lies have no place in democracy. They are of the things that undermine and destroy democracy. There is a limit on how much confusion, doubt and cynicism a polity can tolerate.

Kurt Waldheim was falsely accused and his life affected in a most profound way. In Europe, belief in America and what it should stand for was compromised. The United Nations suffered in America, where it must have decisive support. Austria was criticized for allegedly electing a supposed war criminal as its President. How has that affected Austrian politics? Did it contribute to the rise of extreme conservatism in that nation?

At the very least the allegations charging Dr. Waldheim to have been a Nazi deserve a full review by the Justice Department or an independent entity. The untoward Watch List decision should be rescinded and a formal apology made.

The greater issue, however, is more subtle and insidious. It is the effect on faith in democracy. How could such an act as the attack on Kurt Waldheim ever happen in a reasoned and democratic world? What does it mean to democracy when vicious personal attack is allowed without foundation and virtually sustained by a government? In the Waldheim affair, democracy was subverted. Those who were cynical about Western democracy and its political establishments were made more so.

The greatest contribution that the accusers could now make is to admit their mistake. This will serve the nation in a far greater way than their disservice. They have the opportunity to produce a profound event in American democracy which would set the highest example. Their accusations were unintentional. They believed they were right. By such an act they can call the nation's attention to the ultimate need for truth. This will also preserve the credibility of those who most remind the world of the promise of "never again" since "never again" has repeatedly happened.

If this does not happen then what other lies and false perceptions will be justified by the Waldheim affair? What other interest or advocate groups will perpetrate "big lies" or already have? The prospects are frightening when the number of such groups in the United States and in Europe are considered along with the amount of money they have available. Consider also what political parties and campaign staffs might do if unchecked by the media.

The overriding lesson is that truth and justice are precious in democracy. They are fundamental. There cannot be democracy without them. They must be respected and preserved by all who value freedom. They must never be perverted for reasons of personal or organizational agenda. Truth is the ultimate unifier of a nation. It leads to the solution to most problems. When the media, political leaders, political parties and governments fail to seek, find, and report the truths of issues or when they fail to create clear and comprehensive debate, they abdicate their most crucial responsibility. It is then that the writers, researchers, thinkers, poets and their publishers must mobilize the scientific and historical facts, the relevant analyses, and the new thinking for the people to consider in meaningful debate and dialog before a corrupted government sends its police to stop them.

Gerry Balcar
Chairman and C.E.O.
Olin Frederick, Inc.

NOTES

CHAPTER I

1. See Guenther Ofner, "Die Rolle de SPOE in der Waldheim-Kampagne (The Role of the Austrian Socialist Party in the Waldheim Campaign)," in *Die Kampagne*, F. A. Herbig Verlagsbuchhandlung, Muenchen-Berlin 1987, and Robert Edwin Herzstein, *Waldheim—The Missing Years*, Paragon House, New York, 1989, p.234.
2. Ofner in *Die Kampagne*, pp. 127 and 132; Herzstein, *Waldheim—The Missing Years*.
3. Ofner in *Die Kampagne*, pp. 133-134.
4. *Profil*, Vienna, January 27, 1986; Eli M. Rosenbaum, *Betrayal*, St. Martin's Press, New York, 1993, p.14.
5. Alan Levy, *The Wiesenthal File*, William B. Eerdmans Publishing Company, Grand Rapids, Michigan, 1993, p.400; Simon Wiesenthal, *Justice, Not Vengeance*, Weidenfeld & Nicholson, London, 1989, p. 312. Sinowatz has denied that the Austrian Socialist Party was behind the charges against Waldheim.
6. Rosenbaum, *Betrayal*, pp. 2-8.
7. Ibid.
8. Ibid., pp. 10-50.
9. Ibid., pp. 18-19 and 48-49.
10. Ibid., p 33.
11. *Kurt Waldheim's Wartime Years—A Documentation*, Carl Gerold's Sohn, Vienna, 1987, p. 42. This book was put together and published by the Austrian government as a rebuttal to the allegations against Waldheim. It is discussed in Chapter 4.
12. Rosenbaum, *Betrayal*, p. 58.
13. Ibid., pp. 63-4.
14. Ibid., pp. 73-7.
15. Statements made by Trauttmansdorff to the author during an interview in 1995.
16. *Kurt Waldheim's Wartime Years*, pp. 133-5.
17. Rosenbaum, *Betrayal*, pp. 83-6.
18. John T. McQuiston, "Waldheim Says His Past Was Misrepresented," *The New York Times*, March 6, 1986, p. A6. Waldheim used Fleischer's comments to support his denial of any involvement in Jewish deportations. Apparently Fleischer regretted having made such comments, for he described Waldheim's use of them as a "dirty trick," adding that Waldheim was one of the "best informed" Wehrmacht officers in all of Greece (Rosenbaum, *Betrayal*, p. 215). Alan Levy (The Wiesenthal File, p.374) quotes Fleischer as having also said that "it is even probable that [Waldheim] personally attended executions in Yugoslavia," which Levy considered to be "scholarly overreach" on Fleischer's part. Fleischer later participated in the work of the Historians' Commission (see Chapter 4).
19. Kurt Waldheim, *Im Glaspalast der Weltpolitik*, Econ Verlag, Duesseldorf and Vienna, 1985, p. 42.
20. Rosenbaum, *Betrayal*, p. 31.
21. Ibid., p. 95.
22. *The New York Times*, March 6, 1986, p. A6.
23. "News from the World Jewish Congress," New York, March 5, 1986. An analysis by Esther Schollum of the WJC press campaign against Waldheim appears in *Die Kampagne*, pp. 26-38.

24. William Drodziak, "Waldheim Defends Wartime Record; Surge of Popular Sympathy Bolsters His Presidential Campaign," *The Washington Post*, March 12, 1986, p. A25.
25. Lucien O. Meysels, "Die Akte Waldheim," *Wochenpresse*, Vienna, March 11, 1986.
26. Rosenbaum, *Betrayal*, pp. 114-120.
27. Ibid., pp. 129-136.
28. Ibid., pp. 151.
29. Ibid., p. 91.
30. *Kurt Waldheim's Wartime Years*, p. 74.
31. *New York Newsday*, April 22, 1986, cited by Rosenbaum in *Betrayal*, p. 232.
32. e.g. William Safire and Anthony Lewis in *The New York Times* of April 21, 1986, and May 1, 1986, respectively.
33. *Kurt Waldheim's Wartime Years*, p. 47.
34. See affidavit of Herbert Warnstorff, one of Waldheim's commanding officers, in *Kurt Waldheim's Wartime Years*, p. 203, and *The Waldheim Report* (English translation), International Commission of Historians, Museum Tusculaneum Press, University of Copenhagen, 1993, p. 211.
35. *The New York Times*, May 17, 1986, p. A4; Wiesenthal, *Justice, Not Vengeance*, pp. 314-5.
36. Rosenbaum, *Betrayal*, p. 229.
37. Levy, *The Wiesenthal File*, p. 404; Wiesenthal, *Justice, Not Vengeance*, p. 316.
38. John Tagliabue, "A Tense Time Now For Jews of Vienna," *The New York Times*, April 11, 1986, p. A12.
39. Rosenbaum, *Betrayal*, pp. 156-7.
40. See affidavit of Lord Wiedenfeld in *Kurt Waldheim's Wartime Years*, pp. 101-2.
41. *The New York Times*, April 14, 1986, p. A9.
42. *The New York Times*, May 3, 1986, p. A2.
43. Rosenbaum, *Betrayal*, pp. 266-270; *The New York Times*, May 15, 1986, p. A19.
44. *Associated Press* dispatch, Tel Aviv, May 23, 1986; *The New York Times*, May 23, 1986, p. A9.
45. Ibid.
46. *The New York Times*, June 5, 1986, p. A10
47. Reuters North European Service, Tel Aviv, June 8, 1986; *The New York Times*, June 10, 1986, p. A8.
48. Rosenbaum, *Betrayal*, pp. 283-4.
49. *The New York Times*, June 9, 1986, p. A4.
50. Ibid., June 10, 1986, p. A8.
51. Rosenbaum, *Betrayal*, p. 292.
52. Reuters North European Service, Tel Aviv, June 8, 1986.
53. *The New York Times*, June 19, 1986, p. A5.
54. Ibid., July 2, 1986, p. A6.
55. Ibid., June 10, 1986, p. A27.
56. Ibid., June 12, 1986, p. A31.
57. Rosenbaum, *Betrayal*, p. 152.
58. *The New York Times*, April 29, 1986, p. A14.

CHAPTER II

1. Allan A. Ryan, Jr., *Quiet Neighbors—Prosecuting Nazi War Criminals in America*, Harcourt Brace Jovanovich, New York, 1984, p. 53.
2. 8 USC 1182.
3. Ryan, *Quiet Neighbors*, p. 62.

4. Ibid., p. 249.
5. Ibid., pp. 353-361 (List of cases filed by OSI through July 1984).
6. 8 USC 1182 (a) (33).
7. The account of the Walus case is based primarily on Ryan, *Quiet Neighbors*, pp. 210-217; Michael Arndt, "The Wrong Man," *Chicago Tribune*, December 2, 1984; Flora Johnson, "The Nazi Who Never Was," *The Washington Post*, May 10, 1981; Flora Johnson, "To Catch a Nazi—The Persecution of Frank Walus," *Chicago Reader*, January 23, 1981.
8. Robert Pear, "Israeli Assails Justice Department Decision On Accused Nazi," *The New York Times*, January 26, 1981, p. A19.
9. Ryan, *Quiet Neighbors*, pp. 216-217.
10. The account of the Demjanjuk case is primarily based on Ryan, *Quiet Neighbors*, Chapter 4, "John Demjanjuk: Ivan the Terrible" and Yoram Sheftel, *The Demjanjuk Affair—The Rise and Fall of a Show Trial*, Victor Gollancz, London, 1994 (also published by Regnery Publishing, Inc., Washington D.C., 1996).
11. Ryan, *Quiet Neighbors*, p. 107.
12. United States Court of Appeals for the Sixth Circuit, No. 85-3435, *Demjanjuk v. Petrovsky*, November 17, 1993, p. 27.
13. Sheftel, *The Demjanjuk Affair*, pp. 274-5.
14. See Note 12, supra.
15. Sheftel, *The Demjanjuk Affair*, p. 331.
16. Stephen Labaton, "Justice Dept. Is Pressing U.S. Court to Keep Demjanjuk Out," *The New York Times*, August 19, 1993, p. A8.
17. *Los Angeles Times*, December 31, 1993, p. A16.
18. *The New York Times*, November 22, 1993.
19. Ibid., August, 4, 1993.
20. Ryan, *Quiet Neighbors*, p. 140.
21. The account of the Rudolph case is essentially based on Thomas Franklin, *An American in Exile—The Story of Arthur Rudolph*, Christopher Kaylor Company, Huntsville, Alabama, 1987, which reproduces the transcripts of the various OSI interrogations of Rudolph as well as related documents.
22. Linda Hunt, *Secret Agenda—The United States Government, Nazi Scientists, and Project Paperclip*, 1945 to 1990, St. Martin's Press, New York, 1991, pp. 239-240. Hunt reflects the OSI viewpoint on Rudolph.
23. *Arthur Rudolph v. United States Department of Justice et al.*, United States District Court for the Northern District of California, February 9, 1993, and April 12, 1995.

CHAPTER III

1. Rosenbaum, *Betrayal*, p. 9.
2. This memorandum, as well as the other Justice Department writings mentioned in this chapter, were made public along with the OSI Report in 1994 (see Chapter 7) and are in the author's files.
3. Rosenbaum, *Betrayal*, pp. 236-7.
4. Reminiscences of Donald Santarelli recounted to the author.
5. Ibid.; letter from Santarelli to Attorney General Meese dated May 24, 1986, protesting OSI's unwillingness to consider materials and evidence in defense of Kurt Waldheim.
6. Santarelli submissions of June 11, 1986, and August 1, 1986, including nearly one hundred documentary exhibits; supplementary submissions of November 24, 1986, and December 19, 1986, rebutting new charges made by the WJC, and transmitting an article that appeared in The Jerusalem Post on November 24, 1986, indicating that

the Israeli Ministry of Justice had "no evidence" to link Waldheim to crimes against the Jewish people.

7. Letter from Trott to Santarelli, July 3, 1986.

8. Herzstein, *Waldheim—The Missing Years*, pp. 193-211; 244-246; Rosenbaum, *Betrayal*, p. 366. It is not clear whether the OSI and Austrian investigators had the full access to the Yugoslav archives, that was granted to Herzstein. Rosenbaum made no reference in his book to Herzstein's confirmation that the Yugoslav war-crime charges against Waldheim were fabricated.

9. Memorandum from Sher to Mark Richard, June 27, 1986, reiterating his earlier recommendations that Waldheim be placed on the Watch List and declaring that "there was no point in meeting again with [Waldheim's] attorneys."

10. Former Attorney General Meese has not responded to requests for an interview by the author, and the comments on Meese's reactions and motives are only educated guesses.

11. *The New York Times*, July 4, 1986, p. A4.

12. Rosenbaum, *Betrayal*, pp. 326-7.

13. Marvin Hier and Abraham Cooper, "If the Austrians Elect Waldheim, Bar Him From The U.S." *The New York Times*, May 15, 1986, p. A27.

14. Levy, *The Wiesenthal File*, pp. 413-4.

15. P. B8.

16. April 2, 1987.

17. Kurt Waldheim, *Die Antwort*, Amalthea, Vienna, 1996, p. 146.

18. Rosenbaum, *Betrayal*, p. 392.

19. Former Secretary of State George Shultz has not responded to requests for information by the author.

20. Kurt Waldheim, *Die Antwort*, p. 151-2, confirmed in a letter from Schifter to the author dated December 17, 1996. A more likely explanation for Shultz's failure to oppose the Watch List decision, as would have been normal for the man responsible for the U.S. diplomacy, is that Shultz was simply following orders under a political decision made at the White House level.

21. *The New York Times*, April 28, 1987, p. A1; Rosenbaum, *Betrayal*, p. 393. William P. Clark, a close friend of President Reagan who served in his administration as deputy secretary of state, national security advisor and secretary of the interior, wrote to the author on January 23 and February 21, 1996, that President Reagan learned of the Watch List decision only after it had been announced and was angered both by the decision and by the failure to advise him in advance. Clark had left the government before the Watch List action took place, but he urged several of his former Cabinet colleagues not to take such action, arguing that it would be an unjust act and highly detrimental to relations with Austria, with which he had previously been involved.

22. Rosenbaum, *Betrayal*, p. 394.

23. Joseph Fitchett, *International Herald Tribune*, February 6, 1988.

24. The Austrian Embassy in Washington gave the author copies of the Austrian Government Statement and the note verbale.

25. *Le Soir*, Brussels, June 12, 1987, p. 3.

26. George Archibald and Lou Marano, "Austrian Official Claims U.S. Reneged on Waldheim Data," *Washington Times*, September 30, 1987.

27. Protokoll (Minutes) of May 15, 1987, meeting in Vienna, prepared by Ambassador Helmut Tuerk, Klestil's successor in Washington (in author's file). The account of the meeting is based on this document.

28. Andreas Unterberger, "Aerger in Wien ueber US-Botschafter Ronald Lauder (Anger in Vienna Over U.S. Ambassador Ronald Lauder)," Die Presse, Vienna, May 21, 1987.

29. Rosenbaum, *Betrayal*, p. 327.
30. Waldheim, *Die Antwort*, pp. 187-8.
31. Ibid.
32. *The New York Times*, May 22, 1987, p. 1,3.

CHAPTER IV

1. *Profil*, Vienna, February 15, 1988, p. 22; Jean Vanwelkenhuyzen, "L'affaire Waldheim," *La Revue Generale*, Brussels, August-September 1988, p. 38.
2. *Profil*, ibid.; recollections of Jean Vanwelkenhuyzen, recounted to author.
3. See Vanwelkenhuyzen, *La Revue Generale*, August-September 1988, p. 14 and note to author dated 21 August 1997; Manfred Messerschmidt, Introduction to *The Waldheim Report*, University of Copenhagen, 1993, p.7.
4. Rosenbaum, *Betrayal*, p. 332.
5. Manfried Rauchensteiner, "Der Historikerkommission," *Oestereichisches Jahrbuch fuer Politik* (1988), Vienna, 1989, P. 346.
6. Vanwelkenhuyzen, note to author dated 21 August 1997. Messerschmidt's anti-Waldheim bias is evident in his introduction to the English translation of the Historians' Report, which he edited. The translation itself also shows signs of such bias.
7. Ibid.
8. Rauchensteiner, *Oestereichisches Jahrbuch fuer Politik* (1988), Vienna, 1989, P. 345.
9. Carl Gerold's Sohn Verlag, Vienna.
10. Gen. J. Lawton Collins, Jr., Second Annual James E. O'Neill Lecture, "The Several Investigations of Kurt Waldheim," National Archives, Washington, D.C., February 1990, p.10.
11. Pp. 20-4.
12. Manfred Messerschmidt, Introduction to *The Waldheim Report*, p. 11. The WJC wrote to the Commission, "We must therefore state frankly that the WJC has entertained grave doubts and reservations as regards cooperation with a panel of inquiry unilaterally appointed (sic) and financed by the Government of Austria."
13. Rosenbaum, *Betrayal*, p. 423.
14. Ibid.; Collins, O'Neill Lecture, p. 16-7.
15. Joseph Fitchett, "In the US, Skepticism Over Austrian Inquiry," *International Herald Tribune*, February 6, 1988.
16. *Der Spiegel*, Hamburg, February 1, 1988.
17. *The New York Times*, February 11, 1988, p. A12; Rosenbaum, *Betrayal*, pp. 433-4.
18. Note by Vanwelkenhuyzen in author's files; see also Rosenbaum, *Betrayal*, p. 426 on the WJC position.
19. *The Waldheim Report* (English translation), University of Copenhagen, 1993, pp. 189-205.
20. The Austrian government never published the report, but copies were available through the Austrian Press Office. An English translation was published on the initiative of Messerschmidt.
21. See *The Waldheim Report* (English translation), p.27; original German version, p.1.
22. Ibid., p.65-6; p.72.
23. Ibid., p.95; the English translation erroneously states that Waldheim "became part of the military machine which brought those events about." See p.80 of German version.
24. Ibid., p.200-1.
25. Ibid., p.106; once again, the English translation is inaccurate, referring to "accuracy of content" instead of the German "true copy."

26. Ibid., p.107.
27. Ibid., p.55.
28. See Collins (Note 10 supra) p.23. There is no indication in Wallach's text that Professor Fleischer (who participated in the Commission's deliberations) had come to a similar conclusion in March 1986.
29. *The Waldheim Report* (English translation) p.168.
30. Ibid., pp.177-8.
31. Ibid., pp.17-8; compare with transcript of Waldheim interview, pp.189-206.
32. Vanwelkenhuyzen, *La Revue Generale*, August-September 1988, pp.36-38 and note to author dated August 18, 1997.
33. Vanwelkenhuyzen, *La Revue Generale*, August-September 1988, pp.38-9.
34. Vanwelkenhuyzen, notes to author dated August 18 and 21, 1997.
35. Rosenbaum, *Betrayal*, pp.441-3.
36. Ibid., p.430.
37. Ibid., p.442; Rauchensteiner, *Oesterreichisches Jahrbuch fuer Politik* (1988), 354, who noted that Messerschmidt and Wallach, the "hardliners" on the Commission, were the "stars" of the press conference, which the "neutrals" Collins and Vanwelkenhuyzen did not attend.

CHAPTER V

1. Jack Saltman, *Kurt Waldheim—A Case to Answer?*, Robson Books, London, 1988.
2. Ibid., pp.39-42.
3. Ibid., pp.53-54.
4. Rosenbaum, *Betrayal*, pp.287-9; p.328.
5. Saltman, *Kurt Waldheim—A Case to Answer?*, p.56.
6.. Ibid., p.76
7. Ibid., p.50
8. Ibid., p.100.
9. Ibid., pp.178-9.
10. Information regarding the files can be obtained from the Librarian of the University at University Park, Nottingham NG7 2RD, tel. 01602 514 666.
11. Saltman, *Kurt Waldheim—A Case to Answer?*, p.358.
12. Ibid., pp.355-8.
13. Ibid., p.361.
14. Curiously, Saltman's book does not include the decision of the commissioners. In a letter to the author, Saltman explained that the omission was intended to maintain the element of surprise for the television program, because the book was put on sale the same day as the broadcast. Dr. Ralph Scheide, President Waldheim's personal aide, provided a full transcript of the decision to the author.
15. Saltman, *Kurt Waldheim—A Case to Answer?*, p.366.
16. *Time*, April 25, 1988, p.103
17. June 4, 1988, p.A54.
18. Ibid.
19. Ibid.
20. June 3, 1988.
21. June 5, 1988. p.B33.
22. Ibid., p.D30.
23. *The New York Times*, June 6, 1988, p.C18.

CHAPTER VI

1. Rosenbaum, *Betrayal*, p.279.
2. Ibid.
3. Ibid., p.291
4. International Commission of Historians, *The Waldheim Report* (English translation), p.81. In a second letter, Howe advised Janner that "no evidence was found that Dr. Waldheim was involved" in the fate of a second group of commandos. Rosenbaum, *Betrayal*, p.363-4.
5. *The Waldheim Report* (English translation), p. 209.
6. Ministry of Defence, "Review of the results of investigations carried out by the Ministry of Defence in 1986 into the fate of British servicemen captured in Greece and the Greek Islands between October 1943 and October 1944 and the involvement, if any, of the then Lieutenant Waldheim," Her Majesty's Stationery Office, 1989, Chapter 1, p.1.
7. Ibid., p.2
8. Ibid., piii.
9. Ibid., Legal Background and Assessments, p.8.
10. Waldheim, *Die Antwort*, p. 203.
11. Craig Whitney, "London Discounts Role By Waldheim," *The New York Times*, October 18, 1989.
12. Ibid.
13. Waldheim, *Die Antwort*, p.154.
14. Ibid., p.157.

CHAPTER VII

1. Edgar M. Bronfman, "Shame on Austria," *The New York Times*, June 10, 1986, p.A27.
2. Levy, *The Wiesenthal File*, p.425; Joseph Kaiser, *Im Streit um ein Staatsoberhaupt*, Duncker & Humblot, Berlin, 1988, p.49.
3. *The New York Times*, June 20, 1987, p.A2 and June 26, p.A4.
4. Ibid., June 21, 1987, p.D25.
5. Waldheim, *Die Antwort*, pp.161-2.
6. Ibid., p.160.
7. Henry Grunwald, *One Man's America*, Doubleday, 1997.
8. John Mapother, *Wie man auf die Watchlist kommt*, Ibera & Molden, Vienna, 1997.
9. *John R. Mapother v. Department of Justice*, U.S. District Court for the District of Columbia, Civil Action No. 89-0043.
10. Rosenbaum, *Betrayal*, pp.375-389.
11. Letters dated December 1, 1993, from David Vladeck, of Public Citizen Litigation Group to Marina U. Braswell, assistant United States attorney and to Merrick B. Garland, deputy assistant attorney general, Criminal Division, Department of Justice (copies in author's files).
12. Alan Elsner, "U.S. May Release File on Waldheim's Nazi Past," (Reuters).
13. James Vicini "Waldheim Aided Nazi Persecution," (Reuters).
14. Denis Hevesi, "Report Details Waldheim's Role in Nazi Military," p.A6.
15. Thomas Lippman, "Report Ties Waldheim to Atrocities," p.A1.
16. *In the Matter of Kurt Waldheim*, Office of Special Investigations, Department of Justice, April 9, 1987. p.1.
17. Ibid., p.2.
18. Ibid., p.28.

19. Ibid., p.28.
20. Ibid., p.29.
21. Ibid., p.31.
22. Ibid., pp. 33-4.
23. Ibid., p.43.
24. Ibid., p.62 and p.67.
25. Ibid., pp.71-3; p.24.
26. Ibid., p.94 and p.98.
27. Ibid., pp.101-2.
28. Ibid., p.125.
29. Ibid., p.127.
30. Ibid., p.140.
31. Ibid., p. 144.
32. Ibid., p.150.
33. Ibid., p. 158.
34. Ibid., p. 165.
35. *Protokoll* of May 15, 1987 (see Note 27, Chapter 3, supra), p.10.
36. *In the Matter of Kurt Waldheim*, p. 190.
37. Ibid., pp.191-7.
38. Ibid., p.196.
39. Ibid., p.202.
40. See Note 28, Chapter 3, supra.
41. See Note 15, supra.
42. See Note 14, supra.
43. James Vicini, "U.S. Says Waldheim Units Engaged in Nazi Crimes," Reuters, March 13, 1994.
44. Statement by Justice Department spokesman Carl Stern, as reported by Thomas Lippman (see Note 15, supra).
45. Michael Weisskopf, "Justice Official Named to Head Pro-Israel PAC," *The Washington Post*, February, 11, 1994. Sher left AIPAC in 1996 to work for the WJC on its campaign against the Swiss banks' role in World War II (*The National Journal*, August 3, 1996).
46. See Note 44, supra.
47. Mapother, *Wie man auf die Watchlist kommt*, pp.141-3; Binder personally described this incident to the author.
48. Austrian Press and Information Service, *News From Austria*, "Austria Submits Observations to Justice Department Report on Former Austrian President Kurt Waldheim," April 26, 1994.
49. Information that the Austrian Ambassador to the U.S., Helmut Tuerk, passed to the author by telephone.
50. Letter to author from Martin Eichtinger, Austrian Press and Information Service, Washington, D.C., February 22, 1996.
51. E.g., "Jewish Leaders Decry Papal Honor for Kurt Waldheim," *The Washington Post*, July, 30, 1994, p.B7; Near East Report, September 12, 1994, p.164; Allan Cowell, "Pope's Knighthood for Waldheim Angers Israel" (New York Times News Service), *The San Diego Tribune*, August 7, 1994, p.A25.
52. Letter to Archbishop Agostino Cacciavillan on letterhead of House of Representatives, signed by 14 members of Congress, August 18, 1994.

CHAPTER VIII

1. Levy, *The Wiesenthal File*, p.404.

2. See Chapter 1.
3. Levy, *The Wiesenthal File*, p. 386; *Kurt Waldheim's Wartime Years*, pp.25-6; Jean Vanwelkenhuyzen, *La Revue Generale*, August – September 1988, p. 35.
4. Jean Vanwelkenhuzen, ibid.
5. *Kurt Waldheim's Wartime Years*, pp.137-9, reproducing the report of the Berlin Document Center
6. Herzstein, *Waldheim—The Missing Years*, p.55. At a session of the American Historical Association on December 28, 1988, the minutes indicate that Herzstein emphatically declared that "Waldheim was *not* a Nazi," clearly stressing the *not*.
7. *Kurt Waldheim's Wartime Years*, pp.133-5, reproducing the declaration of the Nazi Gau office. Other testimonials as to the anti-Nazi attitude of the Waldheim family appear at pp.111-5. See also the "declaration" of Jean Vanwelkenhuzen, the historian who examined the Nazi allegations for the International Commission of Historians (reproduced in Waldheim's *Die Antwort*, p.195) in which he described Waldheim as an "Austrian patriot, a convinced Roman Catholic...but not at all a Nazi."
8. George Weidenfeld, *Remembering My Good Friends*, HarperCollins, London, 1995.
9. Ibid., pp.62-4.
10. *Kurt Waldheim's Wartime Years*, p.101-2.
11. E.g., AP dispatch, *San Diego Union-Tribune*, August 20, 1994, p.A10; *New York Daily News*, July 30, 1994; USA Today, January 21, 1994; Jim Hoagland, *Washington Post*, August 23, 1994.
12. Memorandum from Rosenbaum to Bronfman transmitting WJC Interim Report on Kurt Waldheim, June 2, 1986, page 4; Rosenbaum, *Betrayal*, p.xix.
13. Kurt Waldheim, *The Challenge of Peace*, New York, Rawson, Wade Publishers, 1977; original French version published as *Un metier unique au monde*, Paris, Editions Stock, 1977.
14. Letter from Stephen J. Solarz, House of Representatives, November 26, 1980, to UN Secretary General Kurt Waldheim; Waldheim's reply to Solarz, December 19, 1980.
15. Kurt Waldheim, *Die Antwort*, p.100.
16. Kurt Waldheim, *In the Eye of the Storm*, London, Weidenfeld & Nicolson, 1985; Washington, D.C., Adler & Adler, 1986; German version published as *Im Glaspalast der Weltpolitik*, Duesseldorf and Vienna, Econ Verlag, 1985.
17. Ibid., p.42 (German version).
18. Affidavit of Alex MacCormick, senior editor, Weidenfeld & Nicolson, in *Kurt Waldheim's Wartime Years*, pp.269-71.
19. *Kurt Waldheim's Wartime Years*, p. 65.
20. *The New York Times*: March 29, 1986, p.A20; April 19, 1986, p.A26; June 10, 1986 p.A26.
21. *Kurt Waldheim's Wartime Years*, pp. 117-26.
22. Rosenbaum, *Betrayal*, pp.213-14.
23. Wiesenthal, *Justice, Not Vengeance*, pp.318-19.
24. Ibid., p.322.

CHAPTER IX

1. Dominique Audibert, *Le Point*, Paris, February 4, 1995, p.31.
2. See note 17, chapter 3.
3. "Waldheim's Spots Haven't Changed," *New York Post*, June 17, 1996. p.20.
4. Rosenbaum, *Betrayal*, p.6.
5. Kurt Waldheim, *Die Antwort*, p.47.
6. Pp.55-9.

7. Edgar M. Bronfman, *The Making of a Jew*, pp.107 and 115-6.
8. Ibid., p.110
9. A similar question has been raised in connection with a law adopted in France on July 14, 1990, which makes it a crime to contest the reality of crimes against humanity (i.e., the Holocaust) as defined by the Nuremberg Military Tribunal. Prominent French Jewish personalities and organizations promoted the law. Some of the law's sponsors soon regretted the adoption of this extraordinary attack on freedom of thought and expression, for it permitted the revisionists to expound their views in court, which gained them much publicity and caused people to wonder why it was necessary to make history dependent on criminal law.
10. *The New York Times*, June 20, 1997, p.A2.
11. Wiesenthal, *Justice, Not Vengeance*, Chapter 43.
12. Ibid., p.320.
13. April 16, 1992.
14. Herzstein, *Waldheim—The Missing Years*.
15. Ibid., pp.99-101.
16. Ibid., pp.251-2.
17. Rosenbaum, *Betrayal*, Note 10, pp.509-10.
18. David Binder, unpublished article dated March 22, 1994.
19. *Present Tense*, American Jewish Committee, May-June 1987
20. March 29, 1986, p.A20.
21. June 10, 1986, p.A26.
22. June 26, 1987, p.A34.
23. February 12, 1988, p.A34.
24. Reprinted in *International Herald Tribune*, April 1, 1992.
25. February 23, 1988; November 24, 1989; May 24, 1994; August 12, 1994; August 19, 1994.
26. June 25, 1996.
27. May 15, 1986; June 10, 1986; July 9, 1986. An exception was the publication by the *Times* on June 6, 1986, of an article by Gerhard Waldheim defending his father.
28. February 14, 1988.
29. John R. Mapother, "Justice Department Secrecy About Waldheim," July 26, 1992.
30. e.g., "Lending Respectability to a Pariah," editorial, August 9, 1994, on papal knighthood award: "[Waldheim's] outcast state is well-deserved... this one-time uniformed servant of the Nazi onslaught... as unrepentant a figure as Mr. Waldheim ignores history and suggests a terrible blind spot."
31. July 28, 1994, p.A31.
32. December 14, 1997. *The New York Times* did not report Lanto's outburst.
33. Carolyn B. Maloney, "The War Crimes Disclosure Act," *The Stars and Stripes*, September 28, 1996, p.7.
34. *The New York Times*, June 25, 1996.

INDEX

The infamous Podgorica photo, May 23rd, 1943. Lieutenant Kurt Waldheim stands between Italian General Escola Roncaglia and SS General Artur Phleps (holding a brief case and speaking) Waldheim, who spoke Italian, was the interpreter. (*Kurt Waldheim's Wartime Years —A Documentation*)

At their New York home on Sutton Place, Kurt Waldheim, Secretary General of the United Nations with his wife and daughter.

Secretary General Waldheim with President Jimmy Carter at the White House. *(Official White House Photograph)*

At Cancun in 1981 with President Ronald Reagan and Jim Baker. *(Photo by Michael Evans of the White House)*

Nationalsozialistische ⊕ Deutsche Arbeiterpartei

Gauleitung Niederdonau Q...'-'

Personalamt

Abteilung: Politische Beurteilung

Vertraulich!

Unser Zeichen u. Zahl
in der Antwort
unbedingt anführen!

Unser Zeichen: Pe-Sch./C.   Ihr Zeichen:
       32327   P.A. 89/40

Betrifft: **Politische Beurteilung**

[/... 1940

An den
Oberlandesgerichtspräsident,

W i e n , I . ,Justizpalast

Wien, ben .... 2. August 194 0
IX. Wolgasse 10, Fernruf A 19-5-40 bis 47
Telefonschrift: Wien IX, Postamt 66, Postschließfach 199

Name: W a l d h e i m   Kurt

Geburtszeit: 21. 12. 1918   Ort: Wördern

Wohnort: Tulln,   Straße: Wildgasse 10

Der Genannte war,wie sein Vater,ein Anhänger des Schuschnigg Regim
und hat in der Systemzeit durch Angeberei seine Gehässigkeit zu
unserer Bewegung unter Beweis gestellt.

Der Genannte ist nun zum Militärdienst eingezogen und soll sich al
Soldat der deutschen Wehrmacht bewährt haben,sodass die Zulassung
zum Justizdienst von mir nicht abgelehnt wird.

                  H e i l   H i t l e r !
             Der Leiter des Gaupersonalamtes:

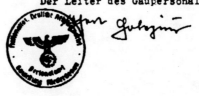

The official Nazi document of August 2nd, 1940 which identifies Kurt Waldheim and his father
as vociferous opponents of Nazism. He is, however, allowed to judicial service as a result of
his military service (and battlefield commission). The translation opposite was done in 1987.
(*Kurt Waldheim's Wartime Years —A Documentation*)

National Socialist German Workers Party
Gauleitung (regional committee) Niederdonau
(Letterhead bearing the symbol of the NSDAP - eagle with swastika)

Personal office
Department: Political assessment
quote our reference
and code in reply!   To the
                                      President of the Regional Court of
                                      Appeals
Confidential!   Vienna, I., Palace of Justice

Our ref: Pe-Sch./C.   Your ref: P.A.89/40
         32327   Vienna, 2nd August 1940.
                                      IX. Wasagasse 10, phone 19550 through 57
                                      post Address: Vienna IX, Postoffice 66,
RE: Political Assessment.   POB 139

Name: W a l d h e i m   Kurt
Date of birth: 21.12.1918   Place of birth: Wördern
Address: Tulln, Street: Wildgasse 10

The above-mentioned was, like his father, a supporter of the Schuschnigg
regime, and during the time of that system gave proof of his spitefulness
towards our movement by boasting.
The above-mentioned has now been conscripted, and is said to have proven
his worth as a soldier of the German Army so that I do not oppose his
admission to judicial service.

                        ·H e i l   H i t l e r !
                    The Head of the Gau Personnel Office:
                    (illegible autographic signature)
Die genaue Übereinstimmung der   (Seal of the NSDAP Gauleitung Niederdonau)
vorstehenden Übersetzung mit der
angehefteten / vorliegenden - Urschrift
Abschrift / Ablichtung bestätige ich
unter Berufung auf meinen Eid.

Wien, am 15.6.1987